101 WOODEN CLOCK PATTERNS

 Joyce R. Novak

Sterling Publishing Co., Inc. New York

DEDICATION

To Lloyd and Laura Kennel, my parents, who have always appreciated the art of fine woodworking.

ACKNOWLEDGMENTS

I wish to thank Eldon and Linda Kennel, my brother and sister-in-law, for all their help and encouragement; Wayne Mink for all his help and time in taking the black-and-white photos; Vicki Rushing, my daughter, for all her help and encouragement; Michael Snider, my attorney, for his expertise; my many friends and customers for their critiques, suggestions, and requests.

Edited by Keith L. Schiffman

Library of Congress Cataloging-in-Publication Data

Novak, Joyce R., 1937–
    101 wooden clock patterns / Joyce R. Novak.
        p.   cm.
    Includes index.
    1. Woodwork.   2. Clocks and watches—Design and construction.
I. Title.   II. Title: One hundred one wooden clock patterns.
III. Title: One hundred and one wooden clock patterns.
TT200.N69   1990
684'.08—dc20   90-9853
                                                CIP

Copyright © 1990 by Joyce R. Novak
Published by Sterling Publishing Company, Inc.
387 Park Avenue South, New York, N.Y. 10016
Distributed in Canada by Sterling Publishing
% Canadian Manda Group, P.O. Box 920, Station U
Toronto, Ontario, Canada M8Z 5P9
Distributed in Great Britain and Europe by Cassell PLC
Villiers House, 41/47 Strand, London WC2N 5JE, England
Distributed in Australia by Capricorn Ltd.
P.O. Box 665, Lane Cove, NSW 2066
Manufactured in the United States of America
All rights reserved

Sterling ISBN 0-8069-5776-X paper

Clock hands pictured on page 125 are reprinted courtesy of KLOCKIT, P.O. Box 636, Lake Geneva, WI 53147.

Clock numerals pictured on page 126 are reprinted courtesy of Precision Movements, 4251 Chestnut St., Emmaus, PA 18049.

Contents

Color Section follows page 64

Preface

I'm someone who likes to stay busy, so I find crafts to be an important part of my life. Crafts have cheered me when I'm lonely, and they have also supplemented my income. I worked for one company for nearly 26 years as a cost accounting clerk. The company went bankrupt in 1984, and, for the first time in my life, I was left without a job to support myself and my teenage daughter. Ten months passed before I found a job which enabled me to support myself and my daughter. During those ten months, I became more involved with the crafts business, and I loved it. I started by crocheting dolls and découpaging pictures. Then I added clocks to the découpaged pictures. At a crafts show one day, I was asked to make a tooth-shaped clock from wood. I made the tooth clock, and then the customer ordered four more!

The tooth-shaped clock opened up a whole new world of ideas for me. Working and creating things from wood had always fascinated me. I began creating patterns and building clocks. At first they were merely stained and varnished silhouettes. Then I decided they needed more character, and I began detailing them with a "hot tool." At crafts shows, many people would come to my booth, stand back and admire the clocks. I would ask, "Do you see something you like?" The answer would be, "Yes, I like them all. I've never seen anything like this before." The customers' responses have been rewarding and encouraging.

My shop started with a few inexpensive tools. Gradually I've been able to add various items and to upgrade equipment to make the job easier and faster. I'm usually very busy, and when I'm not at my office job (I'm a computer operator), you'll find me in my shop.

I trust you'll enjoy using this pattern book to create your own projects.

Joyce R. Novak
Twin Falls, Idaho

Materials and Instructions

I first began to make these clocks as a means to augment my income. Little did I know then that these clocks would become so popular. After showing the clocks at fairs and crafts shows, it clearly became evident that I had the "knack" for designing clocks that had great appeal. Not only are these clocks novel and pretty to look at, but I think that they're easy and fun to make. Even the weekend hobbyist with the barest essentials can make any of these clocks, to the pleasure and admiration of family and friends alike. You'll find a wide range of themes in the patterns here—animals suitable for the nursery, western gear for the "rec room," charming patterns for the kitchen or bath. Thanks to the use of the quartz clock movements, you need never worry about winding or setting the clocks—the movements are accurate and usually need no maintenance. Making these clocks brought me many hours of pleasure. I hope they bring you the same.

These patterns were originally designed for clocks, but they can easily be converted into many other things, such as puzzles, weather vanes, coffee mug holders, towel holders, notepad holders, calendar pad holders, coatracks, necklace holders, etc. Your imagination is the limit. In chapter 16 you will find several of these ideas drawn out for you.

The patterns were designed simply to be wood-burned. However, adding a little color makes many of them more attractive. Suggestions for painting, stencilling or découpage are included in the instructions. You'll find the patterns versatile and fun to work with.

Any kind of wood may be used. Pine is soft and fairly easy to work with. The clocks shown here are made with ¾″ pine. Some of the clocks are wider than the 12″ lumber, so you will need to match the grain as closely as possible and glue the pieces together with carpenter's glue. Be sure to let the glue dry thoroughly overnight before working with the lumber. Remember that 1″ × 12″ lumber is usually 11¾″ wide. You may want to enlarge or reduce some patterns so that they fit on the 11¾″ lumber.

There are several ways to enlarge or reduce a pattern. The easiest and most accurate way is to use a photocopier with variable reduction and enlargement features. The dimensions of the ¾″ pine (noted on each pattern) serve as suggested sizes to help you get started. You will need to enlarge most patterns. The patterns in this book are approximately 5¾″ × 7″. The grids are ½″ square. By using a photocopier's 150% enlargement setting, for example, you will get an 8⅝″ × 10½″ enlargement. Enlarging this copy *again*, at 125% will give you a 10¾″ × 13⅛″ enlargement. You can also enlarge the patterns using the ½″ grid that is part of each pattern. Copy the design square-by-square on larger (or smaller) grid paper with exactly the same number of squares using any enlargement/reduction ratio desired. If a pattern in this book is approximately 5¾″ × 7″, and you want your pattern to be 11½″ × 14″, then draw 1″ squares on your final pattern. You may adjust the size of any pattern to suit your needs or desires. You can also reverse a pattern by "flopping" it, or you can crop a pattern by using just a portion of it.

Inexpensive projectors can enlarge drawings, patterns, and plans. These machines project sharp images onto walls, wood, paper, fabric, or screens. Place the original pattern in the glass tray, switch on the projector, focus and trace. Some projectors enlarge up to 25 times, and can project even three-dimensional objects.

You will be able to find the clock hardware (movement, hands, multicolor clock faces) in crafts supply stores. Clock kit companies advertise in the wood and hobby magazines. They will supply hardware through mail order.

Clock hands are available in several finishes and sizes. The clock hands pictured here have a black or brass finish. The clock kits available have a wide range of clock hand sizes, ranging from 1 7/16" in length to over 4" in length. Remember to choose a set of hour and minute hands that are the appropriate size for the clock face and the wood piece. You don't want to have the hands project beyond the clock itself, nor do you want hands that are so short as to be useless. The second ("sweep-second") hand should be approximately the same length as (or slightly shorter than) the minute hand. Some examples of clock hands are shown in Illus. 44 in the supplies section in the back of this book.

Adhesive-backed numerals are also available from clock kit suppliers. They too come in a wide range of sizes, ranging from 3/8" to 1" in height. You generally have a choice of Roman or Arabic numerals. You may want to substitute dots or bars for the numerals, or just use numerals at the 12, 3, 6, and 9 positions, and use the dots or bars to mark the other hours. The numerals are also pictured in Illus. 45 in the supplies section.

Once you have picked your pattern and hardware, you can make the clock by using the equipment below, and by following the step-by-step directions that follow.

Equipment and Tools You Will Need:
Scroll saw, band saw or jigsaw
Hand drill and assorted bits
Drill press
3" Forstner bit
Belt sander
Finish sander pad
Oscillating sander
Pliers

Hex nut driver
Hammer
Phillips screwdriver
3/4" pine stock
Sawtooth hangers
Wood stains
Wood sealer
Varnish (for use with acrylic paints)
Sandpaper (150, 220, 320, 400 grits)
Wood-burning ("hot") tool
Carpenter's glue

Painting Supplies
Acrylic craft paints in various colors
Number '0' round brush
Flat brushes (Numbers 2, 4, 6, 8)
Number '00' liner brush
2" sponge brush

Clock Hardware
Ultra-thin quartz clock movement
Clock hands
Adhesive-backed numerals
AA batteries
Ready-made multicolor clock faces

Some patterns call for additional parts or supplies
Teddy Bear with Heart (p. 39):
   1/4" wood dowel, 6" long
Butterfly (p. 43):
   Two 6" lengths of brass wire for the antennas
Skier on Sun (p. 79):
   Two 1 1/4" flat head screws
Bowling Ball and Three Pins (p. 87):
   11" gold-tone chain
   2 small gold-tone eye screws
Duck Coatrack (p. 116):
   Two 1 1/2" screws
   Two 1/2" hole plugs
   Three 3 1/2" Shaker pegs
Unicorn Necklace Holder (p. 117):
   5 tie holder pegs
Musical Staff Coffee Mug Holder (p. 118):
   Five 3 1/2" mug pegs
Kitten Note (or Calendar) Pad Holder (p. 119):
   2 bolts and wing nuts
   3" × 5" notepad or 10 5/8" × 8 1/4" calendar pad
   13" × 19" × 3/4" pine calendar holder

Instructions
Trace an outline of the clock pattern onto the wood (Illus. 1). Mark the spot to drill the hole for the clock shaft. Saw out the piece, following the line

you just traced. Use a scroll saw, band saw, or jig-saw (Illus. 2). In general, you can place the pattern on the wood with the grain going whichever way you wish, except for those patterns that call for the grain to run in a particular direction. These patterns are specifically marked.

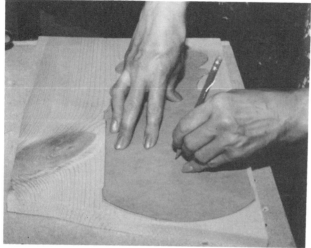

Illus. 1. Tracing the outline and marking the hole for the clock shaft.

Next, sand the edges, using a grinder/sander or a sanding belt attached to a band saw (Illus. 3), or you could sand the piece by hand (Illus. 4). Drill a pilot hole (using a small bit) from the front side, in the spot you marked for the clock shaft (Illus. 5).

Use a Forstner bit to drill a 3″ diameter hole approximately ⅜″ deep on the back side of the wood piece. The quartz clock movement will eventually be placed here. You needn't drill a *circular* hole in the wood piece to keep the clock movement in place. You could make your own template to rout out the back of the piece to the exact dimensions of the clock movement (Illus. 6). Three-inch bits are available for use with a drill press. If you don't have a drill press, you could use a brace and a bit, or a hole saw and a chisel. Now drill a ⁵⁄₁₆″ hole through the middle of the drilled hole (from the front side) for the clock movement shaft (Illus. 7).

Sand the wood piece thoroughly until it is smooth. Sand both sides using a coarse grade sandpaper, about 150 grit (Illus. 8), and then finish with a fine grade sandpaper, about 220 grit (Illus. 9). *Always* sand *with* the grain of the wood. Any scratch marks will appear after varnishing. Next, use a 220 grit sandpaper to take the sharp edges off the top side of the wood piece (Illus. 10).

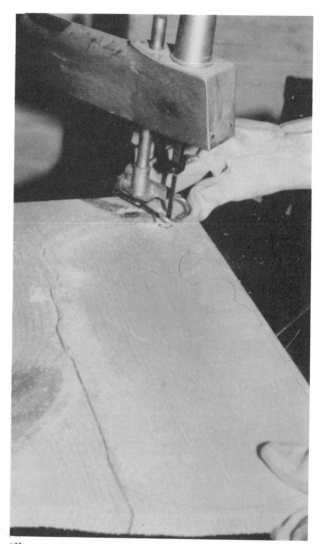

Illus. 2. Sawing out the wood piece.

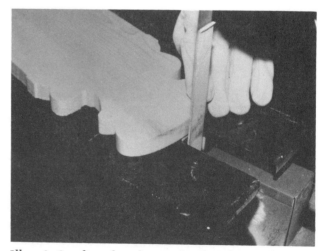

Illus. 3. Sanding the edges with a grinder/sander.

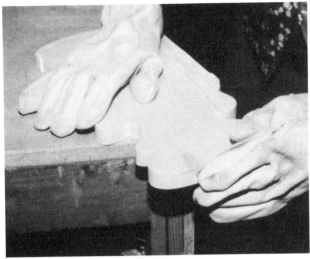

Illus. 4. Sanding the edges by hand.

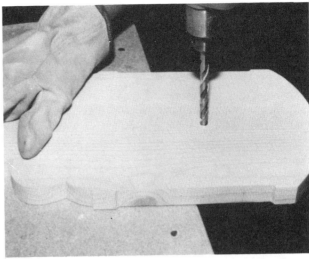

Illus. 7. Drilling the ⁵⁄₁₆″ hole for the clock shaft.

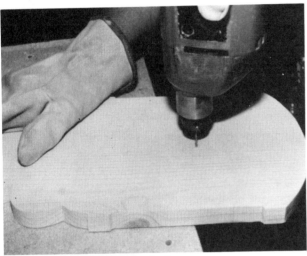

Illus. 5. Drilling the pilot hole.

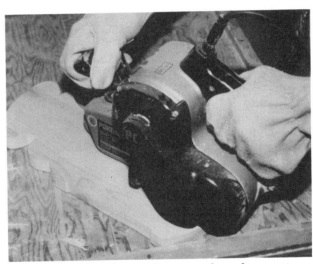

Illus. 8. Sanding the wood piece with medium grit sandpaper.

Illus. 6. Drilling the hole for the quartz clock movement.

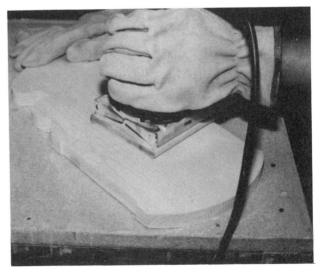

Illus. 9. Sanding the wood piece with fine grit sandpaper.

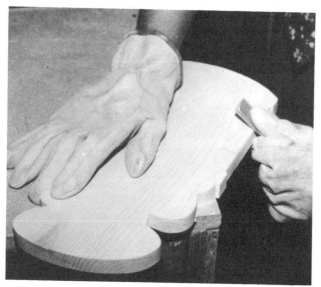

Illus. 10. Taking the sharp edges off the top side of the wood piece.

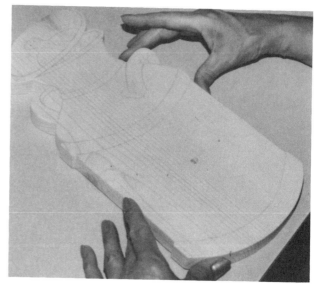

Illus. 12. Wood piece with pattern traced on it.

Trace the detailed pattern lightly onto the wood piece by placing any type of carbon paper between the pattern and the wood piece (Illus. 11 and 12). Carefully follow all the traced lines with the wood-burning tool to detail (Illus. 13 and 14). If you have never used the "hot tool" before, first practice on a scrap piece of lumber to get a feel for the tool. Wood-burning is fun and easy. Anyone can learn to do it.

After the wood piece is wood-burned and detailed, sand it again with 320 grit sandpaper to remove pencil marks, ashes, and sap (Illus. 15).

Stains take differently on different woods. Before staining the detailed wood piece, test the color on scrap lumber. For the clocks pictured here, an "American walnut" stain was used. Using a soft cloth, stain the wood piece to your liking (Illus. 16

Illus. 13. Wood-burning the details.

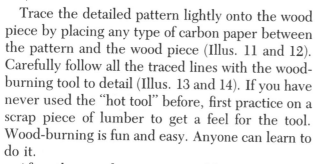

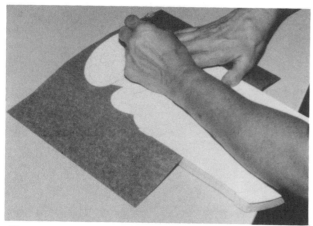

Illus. 11. Tracing the detailed pattern onto the wood piece.

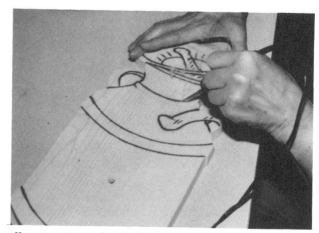

Illus. 14. More details have been wood-burned.

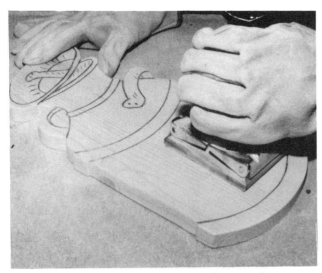

Illus. 15. Sanding with 320 grit sandpaper after wood-burning.

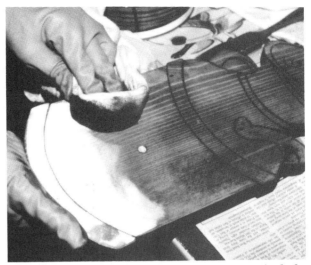

Illus. 17. Staining the wood piece, using a soft cloth. Remember to let the stain dry thoroughly, usually about 8–12 hours.

and 17). Let the stain dry thoroughly, approximately 8 to 12 hours.

Next, seal the wood piece. Follow the directions on the can of sealer. Sand the wood piece lightly using a 220 grit sandpaper. Now varnish the wood piece, following the instructions provided by the manufacturer of the product you are using. Use a good quality varnish and brush (Illus. 18 and 19). Let the varnish dry between coats, according to the manufacturer's suggestions. Sand between coats, using 400 grit sandpaper. Wipe with a damp cloth. If you decide to paint the wood piece, or if you apply stencils or découpage, apply one coat of varnish before and then one or two after. Sand between coats of varnish. If you're not applying "special" finishes, just apply three coats of varnish.

Illus. 18. The piece is ready to be sealed and varnished.

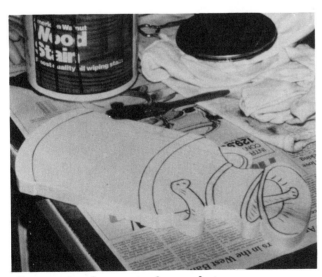

Illus. 16. Ready to stain the wood piece.

Illus. 19. Varnishing with a good-quality brush.

MATERIALS AND INSTRUCTIONS

Find the center of balance by dangling the piece in front of you, holding it between your thumb and index finger. Nail a sawtooth hanger to that "center" spot on the back of the wood piece (Illus. 20).

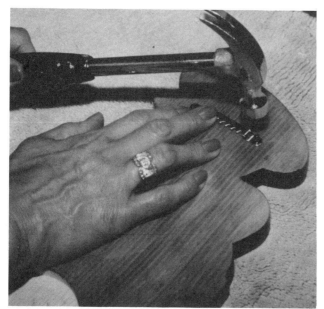

Illus. 20. Nailing the sawtooth hanger on the center of balance.

Put the shaft of the clock movement through the 5/16" hole, and then fasten it using the washer and the hex nut provided with the clock movement kit. Tighten both until the movement is snug, but don't overtighten them (Illus. 21 and 22).

The template will allow you to place all twelve numerals on the clock face accurately, and to create clock faces of varying diameters. The diameter of

Illus. 21. Inserting the quartz clock movement. The clock shaft should fit through the 5/16" hole.

Illus. 22. Tightening the washer and the hex nut.

the clock face depends upon the size of the finished clock. Choose numerals that fit the clock face.

Cut the clock face template to the desired size for the clock dial, and then apply the adhesive-backed numerals. Place each numeral at an intersection of a radiating spoke and a circle (Illus. 23).

Illus. 23. The template is used to position the numbers on the clock face.

Using the minute hand, turn the clock movement shaft to 12 (the slot on the minute hand and the slot on the shaft should line up); then remove the minute hand, and slide the hour hand onto the shaft, pointing it to 9. The hour hand fits rather tight on the shaft, but keep working it down until it touches the threaded part of the shaft. Now, put the minute hand on (it will slip into the small hole in the clock movement shaft), pointing it to 12 (which you just preset), and then put on the tiny

Illus. 24. Putting the three clock hands in place.

nut. Tighten the nut. Press the second ("sweep-second") hand on top of the minute hand (Illus. 24). The second hand will slip into the small hole in the clock movement shaft.

Mini-quartz clock movements are excellent and accurate timekeepers. Add one AA battery and then set the time. The clock is now complete (Illus. 25).

If you decide to use multicolor clock face components, you will need to rout the 3″ hole for the clock movement ½″ deep, instead of ⅜″ deep. This allows for the clock movement shaft to extend an extra ⅛″ through the front of the clock. The clock hands will then clear the multicolor clock face component.

Illus. 25. The completed clock.

Finishing

Other than the standard finish previously described (stain, seal and varnish), you could do any of three things to finish the wooden clock.

Painting

You'll need a good selection of acrylic craft paints in various colors, a liner brush (Number '00'), several flat brushes, one round brush (Number '0'), and one 2″ sponge brush. See the materials list at the beginning of this chapter for a full list of supplies.

The instructions for most of the wooden clock patterns in this book include tips for painting. There are nine illustrations included here to show you how to paint your wooden clock. The tips also include directions for painting *and* wood-burning. The "hot tool" is generally used to outline certain areas to be painted. To paint eyes for the various animals, see Illus. 26–29. To paint borders, see Illus. 30. To paint various details (nostrils, eye details, etc.), see Illus. 31. To paint horses' manes, see Illus. 32. To paint animals' ears, see Illus. 33. To paint line details, see Illus. 34.

Illus. 26. Wood-burn the outline of the eye only. Paint a circle for the iris black. Paint the sclera white. Paint the pupil white with a comma or a dot.

Illus. 27. Wood-burn the outline of the eye. The lashes may be wood-burned or painted. Paint the eye black. Paint a white upside-down comma on one side and place a white dot on the other side. Float rouge on the bottom side of the wood-burned line under the eye.

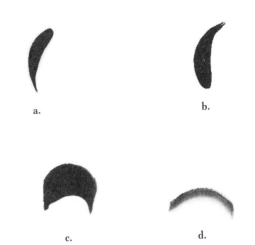

Illus. 28. Wood-burn a circle. Paint the larger portion white. Paint the smaller portion black. Place a white dot in the center of the black portion.

Illus. 31. (a.) Comma (b.) Upside-down comma (c.) "C" stroke (d.) Float

Illus. 29. Wood-burn the outline of the eye and the circle. Paint the circle black for the eyeball. Float tan around the outside of the eye. Float brown on one side of the eyeball, and white on the other side.

Illus. 30. This is a comma and dot border. The commas may be one color, and the dots another color, or both may be painted the same color.

Illus. 32. Wood-burn the mane and the tail. Load a flat brush with black and side-dip the brush in tan. Place the chisel edge of the brush at the top of the mane (or tail) and pull it down in contour with the wood-burned lines.

Illus. 33. Wood-burn the outline and/or the inside of the ear. Float the paint (generally tan or pink) on the inside of the ear or the underside of wood-burned line.

Stencilling

An attractive border motif, or any repetitive pattern can be stencilled. You can use a ready-made stencil, or you can make one of your own design.

Découpage

By using découpage, you can put any of your favorite photographs, news clippings, greeting cards, or any such material onto the clock face. Suggestions for découpage are included with several of the patterns. Some special products used with découpage can be used in place of a varnish finish. These products not only glue down the découpage piece, but also provide a clear, glossy finish.

Illus. 34. Use lighter colors when floating on the upper side of the line. Use darker colors when floating on the underside of the line.

Safety

When using power machinery, be alert. The band saw blade teeth should point *downwards* towards the table; make sure blade tension and blade tracking are both properly adjusted; keep hands and fingers away from the blade; make escape cuts; turn the machine off before removing scrap pieces from the table. Whether sawing or sanding, don't wear jewelry or loose clothing; tie back long hair; hold material firmly; wear a face shield or safety glasses; wear dust and filter masks, especially when sanding; keep your machine and work area as clean as possible.

The wood-burning ("hot") tool should be handled with care. Never place it near flammable material (rags, sawdust, paper). Unplug the tool when you're finished with it; don't leave it on when you're doing something else. Place the hot end on some type of stand when you put it down for a moment. As with all electrical appliances, make sure the tool is in a grounded socket, and avoid shocks. Read the manufacturer's label and warnings before you use the tool.

Metric Equivalents

INCHES TO MILLIMETRES AND CENTIMETRES
MM—millimetres   *CM—centimetres*

Inches	MM	CM	Inches	CM	Inches	CM
⅛	3	0.3	9	22.9	30	76.2
¼	6	0.6	10	25.4	31	78.7
⅜	10	1.0	11	27.9	32	81.3
½	13	1.3	12	30.5	33	83.8
⅝	16	1.6	13	33.0	34	86.4
¾	19	1.9	14	35.6	35	88.9
⅞	22	2.2	15	38.1	36	91.4
1	25	2.5	16	40.6	37	94.0
1¼	32	3.2	17	43.2	38	96.5
1½	38	3.8	18	45.7	39	99.1
1¾	44	4.4	19	48.3	40	101.6
2	51	5.1	20	50.8	41	104.1
2½	64	6.4	21	53.3	42	106.7
2	76	7.6	22	55.9	43	109.2
3½	89	8.9	23	58.4	44	111.8
4	102	10.2	24	61.0	45	114.3
4½	114	11.4	25	63.5	46	116.8
5	127	12.7	26	66.0	47	119.4
6	152	15.2	27	68.6	48	121.9
7	178	17.8	28	71.1	49	124.5
8	203	20.3	29	73.7	50	127.0

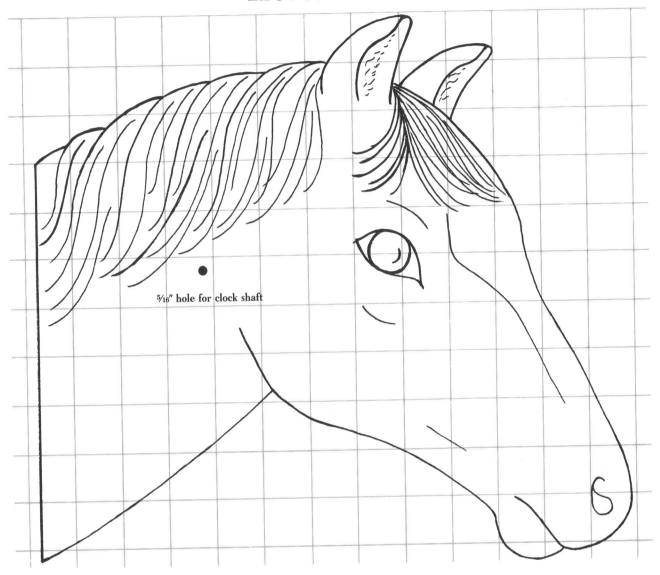

Approximate dimensions: 12¾″ × 11¼″. Scale: ½″ = 1″.

5/16″ hole for clock shaft

Alternate finish

Paint the center of the eye black. Float brown on the right side of the eyeball and white on the left side. Using a flat brush, paint the mane by filling the brush with black paint; side-dip it in tan. Place the chisel edge at the top of the mane, and pull it towards the ends, following the contour of the wood-burned lines. Float tan on the inside of the ear.

Galloping Horse

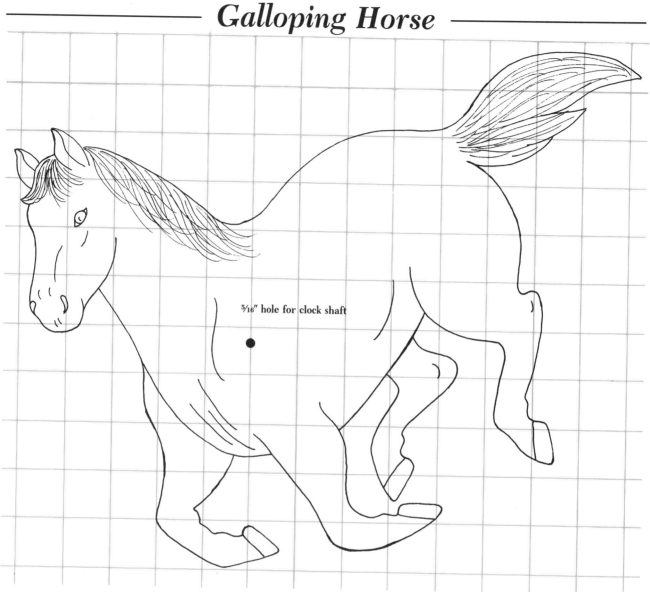

5/16" hole for clock shaft

Approximate dimensions: 14" × 12". Scale: ½" = 1".

Alternate finish

Paint the center of the eye black. Float brown on the lower left side of the eyeball, and white on the upper right side. Using a flat brush, paint the mane by filling the brush with black paint; side-dip it in tan. Place the chisel edge at the top of the mane, and pull it towards the ends following the contour of the wood-burned lines. Do the same with the tail, starting at the body and pulling to the tip of the tail. Float tan on the inside of the ears. Paint the hooves black.

5/16" hole for clock shaft

Approximate dimensions: 18⅛" × 12¾".

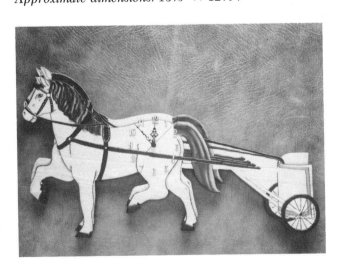

Alternate finish

Paint the center of the eye black. Float brown on the left side of the eyeball and white on the right side. Using a flat brush, paint the manes by filling the brush with black paint, side-dip it in tan. Place the chisel edge at the top of the mane, pull it towards the ends, following the contour of the wood-burned lines. Do the same with the tails, starting at the body and pulling to the tip of the tails. Paint the hooves black. Float tan on the inside of the ears. Using the No. 2 brush, paint the harness and bridles black. Decorate it with gold dots. Paint the chariot a bright color and decorate it with black or white lines around the edges. Paint the wheels black, the axle and the rod (from chariot going between the horses) grey.

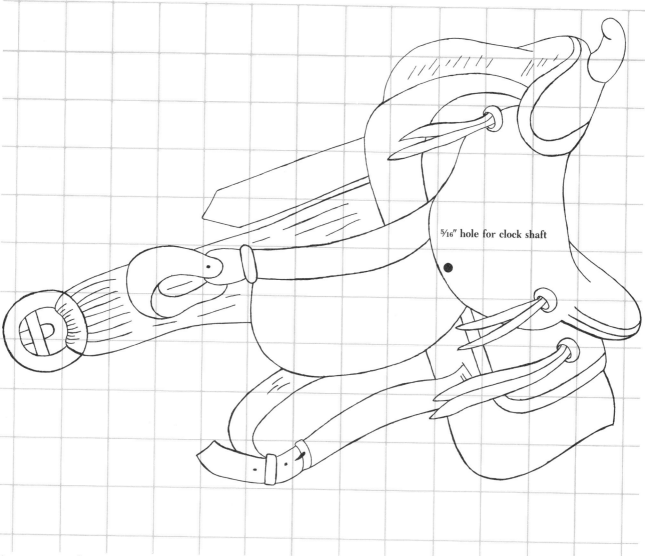

5/16" hole for clock shaft

Approximate dimensions: 15¾" × 10⅛".
Scale: ½" = 1⅛".

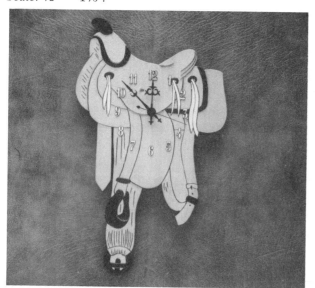

Alternate finish
Paint the stirrup and the rings around the straps black; paint the straps and the cinch ivory.

Cowboy Hat and Spur

⁵⁄₁₆″ hole for clock shaft

Approximate dimensions: 14¾″ × 8″. Scale: ½″ = 1″.

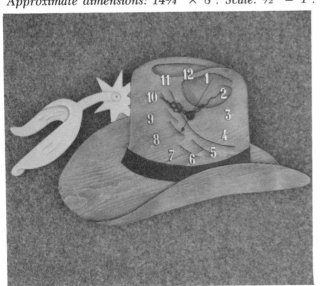

Alternate finish
Paint the spur grey. Paint the band around the hat black.

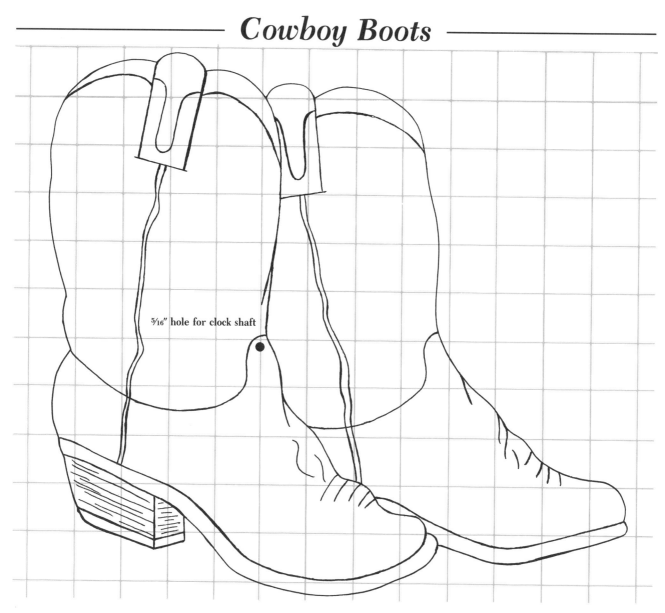

5/16" hole for clock shaft

Approximate dimensions: 12½" × 11¼". Scale: ½" = 1".

Alternate finish

To make the boots look newer, paint the soles and the thin stripe on the side of the boots black.

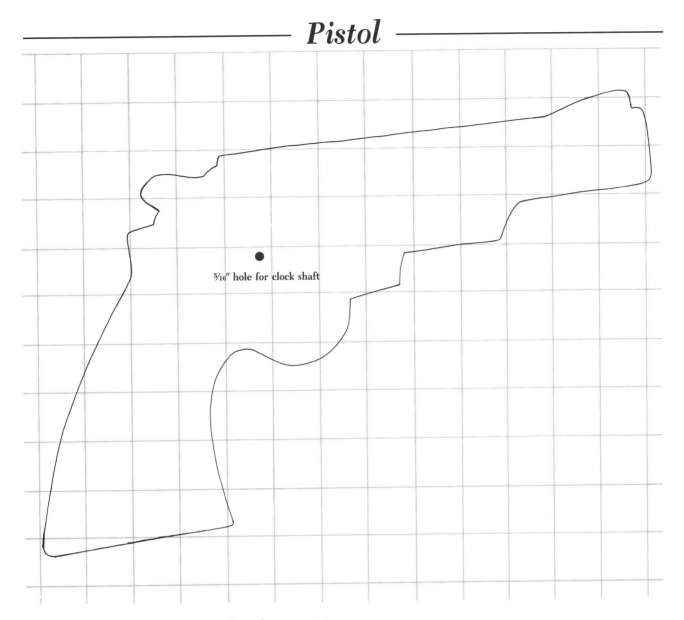

5/16″ hole for clock shaft

Approximate dimensions: 19″ × 12⅜″. Scale: ½″ = 1⅜″.

Alternate finish
Rout the 3″ hole ½″ deep. Use the police car multicolor clock face in place of numbers.

Mermaid

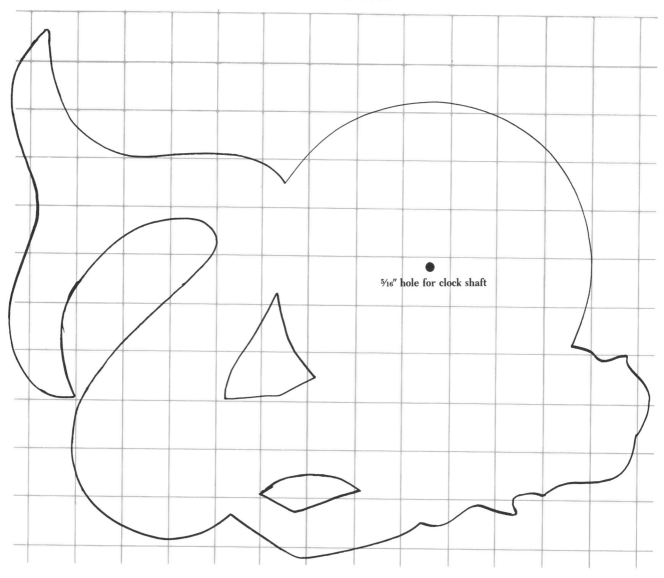

Approximate dimensions: 11″ × 14″. Scale: ½″ = 1″.

5/16″ hole for clock shaft

Alternate finish
Rout the 3″ hole ½″ deep. Use the fish multicolor clock face in place of numbers.

Unicorn

5/16" hole for clock shaft

Approximate dimensions: 13" × 12". Scale: ½" = 1".

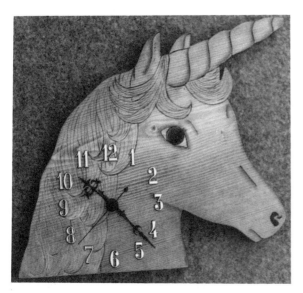

Alternate finish

Paint the center of the eye black. Float brown on the right side of the eyeball, and white on the left side. Float tan on the inside of the ears. Highlight the horn and mane by floating white on the left edge of the wood-burned lines on the horn, and the random upper edges of the wood-burned lines on the mane.

Unicorn on a Heart

5/16" hole for clock shaft

Approximate dimensions: 13" × 10½. Scale: ½" = 1".

Alternate finish

Paint the unicorn white; paint the eye black with a small white comma. Fill a No. 6 flat brush with grey paint. Placing the chisel edge of the brush at the base of the mane, pull it outward to the ends of the mane. Do the same with the tail starting at the body. Paint the hooves grey and the horn antique white.

Dinosaur

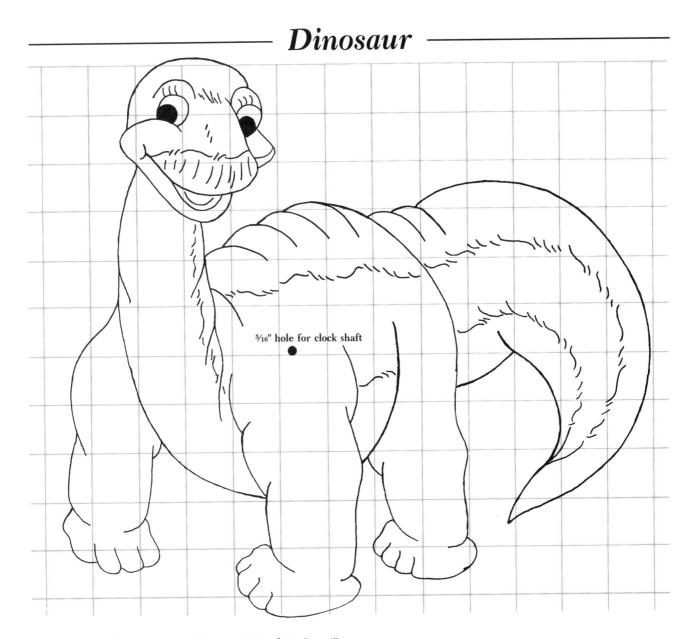

⁵⁄₁₆″ hole for clock shaft

Approximate dimensions: 12½″ × 11½″. Scale: ½″ = 1″.

Alternate finish

Paint the eye black; float coral on the tongue; paint the nose dark brown; float the neck, the underside of the body and the tail with tan.

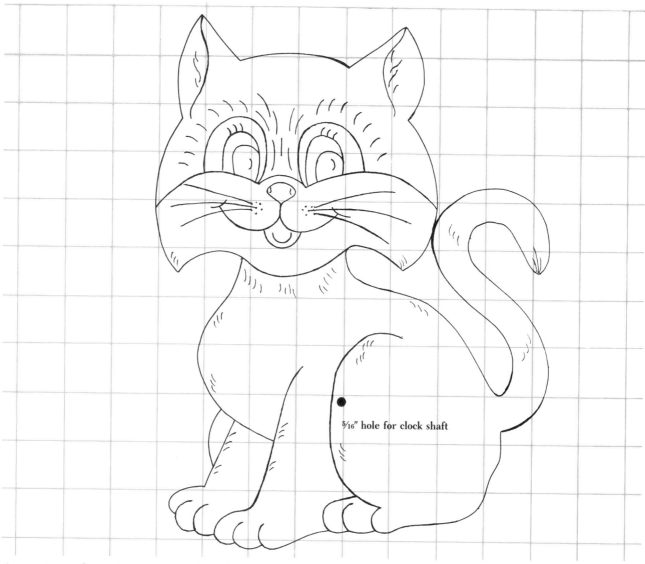

Approximate dimensions: 13¾" × 10½".
Scale: ½" = 1¼".

⁵⁄₁₆" hole for clock shaft

Alternate finish

Paint the center part of the eye black. Paint a white comma on the left side of the eye and a dot on the lower right side. Paint the nose black with tiny commas for nostrils. Float the inside of the ears with pink or tan.

Puppy with Ball

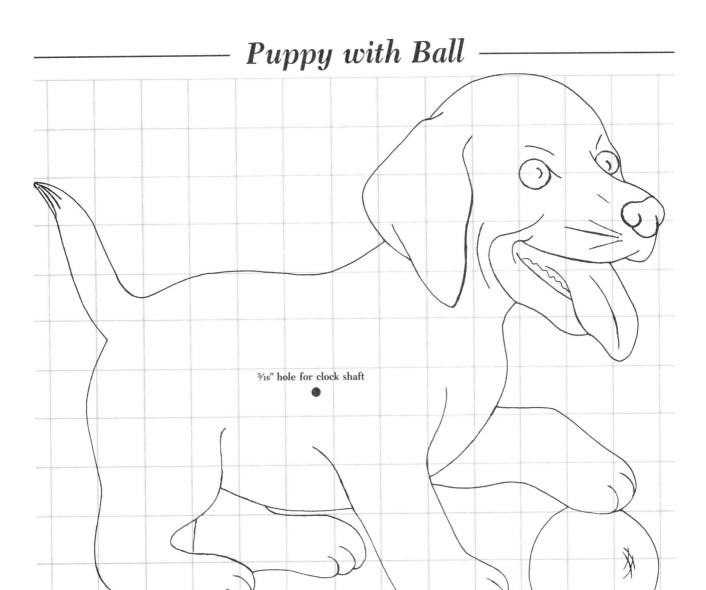

5/16" hole for clock shaft

Approximate dimensions: 12¼″ × 10″. Scale: ½″ = ⅞″.

Alternate finish

Paint the eyes black. Float brown on the right side of the eyeball and white on the left side. Paint the nose black and dark brown, use a comma for the nostril. Paint the tongue coral, the teeth ivory and the ball red.

Bulldog

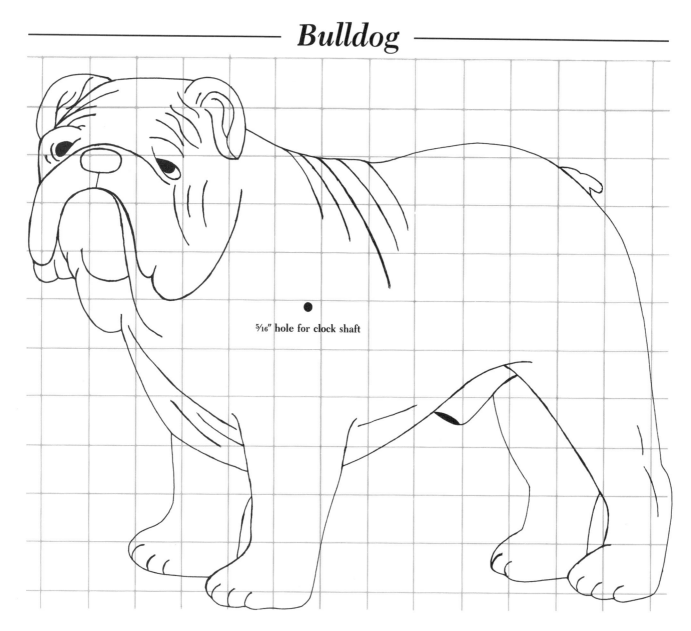

⁵⁄₁₆″ hole for clock shaft

Approximate dimensions: 12¼″ × 10″. Scale: ½″ = ⅞″.

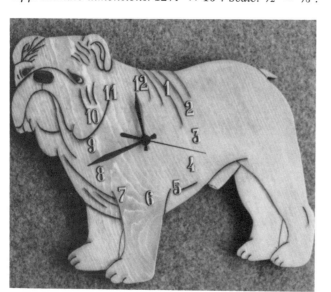

Alternate finish
Paint the eyes black with a small white comma; paint the nose black. Float tan on the inside of the ears, and the upper edge of the wood-burned lines going across the nose and mug.

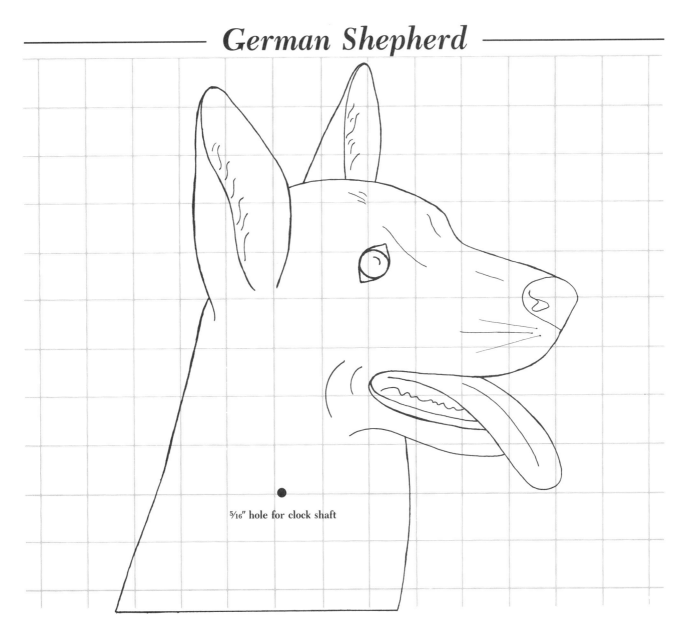

⁵⁄₁₆″ hole for clock shaft

Approximate dimensions: 11¼″ × 13″. Scale: ½″ = 1⅛″.

Alternate finish

Paint the center of the eye black. Float brown on the upper right side of the eyeball and white on the lower left side. Paint the nose black with a dark brown comma for the nostril. Paint the tongue coral and the teeth ivory. Float tan on the inside of the ears.

5/16" hole for clock shaft

Approximate dimensions: 17½" × 12½".
Scale: ½" = 1¼".

Alternate finish

Paint the center of the eyes black. Float brown on the right side of the eyeballs and white on the left side. Paint the nose black with dark brown commas for nostrils.

Mouse

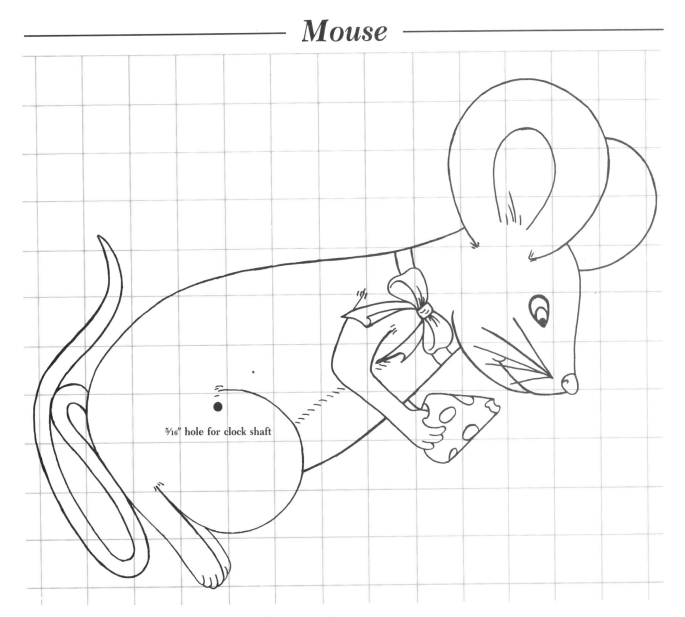

5/16" hole for clock shaft

Approximate dimensions: 9¼" × 14". Scale: ½" = 1".

Alternate finish

Paint the cheese yellow-orange. Float burnt orange on the upper inside edges of the holes in the cheese, white on the lower inside edges. Paint the bow blue. Float pink on the inside of the ear. Paint the nose pink with small white commas for nostrils.

Playful Mouse

straight grain of wood

⁵⁄₁₆″ hole for clock shaft

Approximate dimensions: 11½″ × 12½″. Scale: ½″ = 1″.

Alternate finish and special instructions
Trace the pattern on the wood with the grain running in the direction indicated on the pattern. Paint the cheese yellow-orange and float burnt orange on the upper inside edge of the holes, and white or ivory on the lower inside edges. Paint the center of the eyes white with a large black dot for the pupils. Paint the teeth ivory. Float red on the tongue. Float pink on the inside of the ears.

101 WOODEN CLOCK PATTERNS

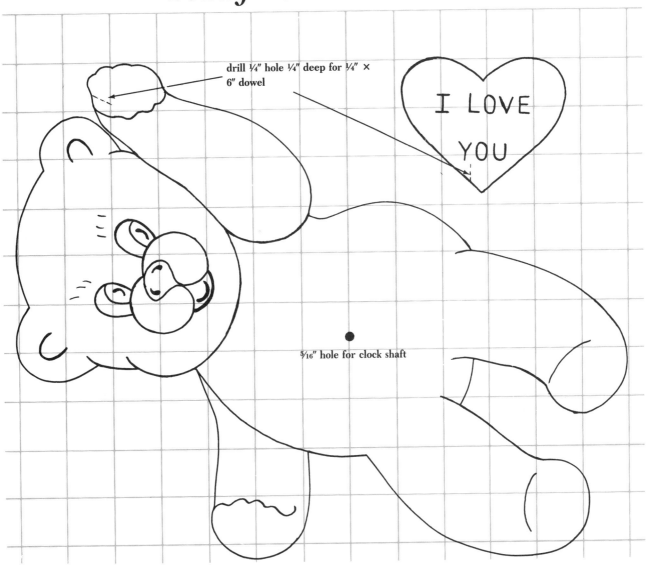

drill ¼″ hole ¼″ deep for ¼″ × 6″ dowel

I LOVE YOU

⁵⁄₁₆″ hole for clock shaft

Approximate dimensions: 8½″ × 14″. Scale: ½″ = 1″.

Alternate finish and special instructions

Drill holes for a ¼″ dowel (6″ long) in the teddy bear's paw, and in the heart, as shown in the pattern. Paint the eyes black with white commas. Paint the muzzle cream and the nose black with small white commas for the nostrils. Float red on the mouth. Dry-brush the cream color inside the ears and on the paws. Paint the heart red.

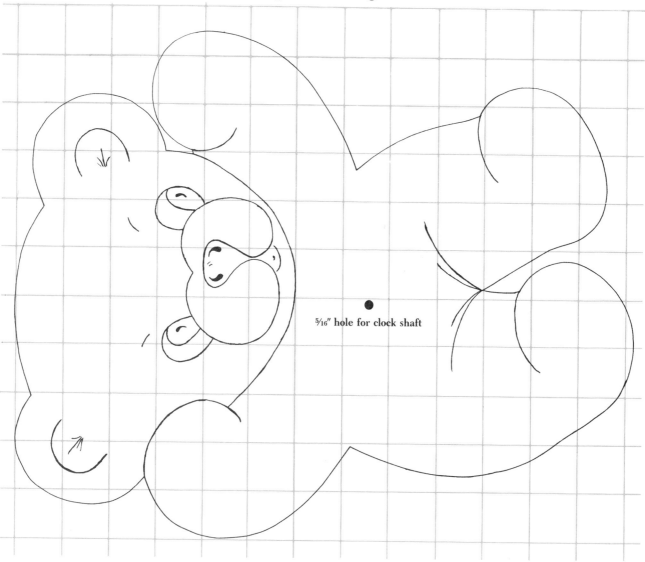

5/16" hole for clock shaft

Approximate dimensions: 9½" × 13¼". Scale: ½" = 1".

Alternate finish
Paint the eyes black with white commas on the right sides of the eyes and a dot on the lower left sides. Paint the muzzle cream and the nose black, with small white commas for the nostrils. Float red on the mouth. Dry-brush the cream color inside the ears and on the paws.

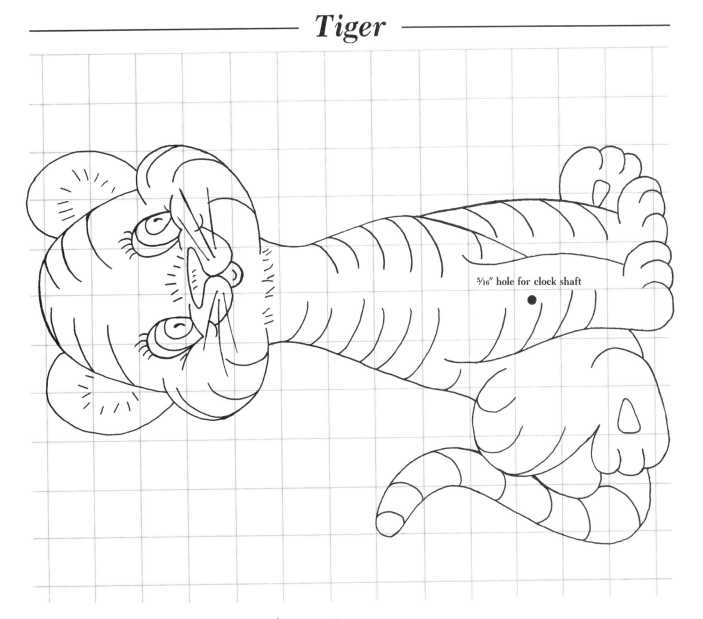

5/16" hole for clock shaft

Approximate dimensions: 13¾" × 8¼". Scale: ½" = 1".

Alternate finish

Paint the center of the eyes green and add a black comma stroke. Paint the nose and the pads on the feet black. Paint small white commas on the nose for the nostrils. Float red on the inside of the mouth. Float pink on the inside of the ears.

Elephant

⁵⁄₁₆″ hole for clock shaft

Approximate dimensions: 11″ × 11″. Scale: ½″ = 1″.

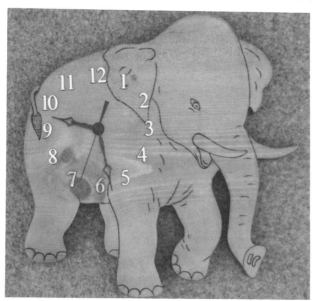

Alternate finish
Paint the tusks ivory. Float red on the mouth and black on the inside of the right side of the nostrils. Paint the toes ivory.

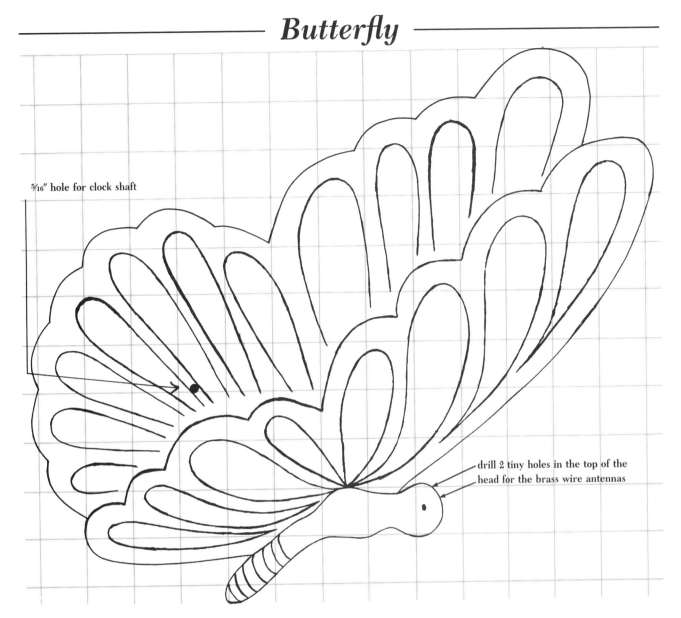

5⁄16″ hole for clock shaft

drill 2 tiny holes in the top of the
head for the brass wire antennas

Approximate dimensions: 9½″ × 14½″. Scale: ½″ = 1″.

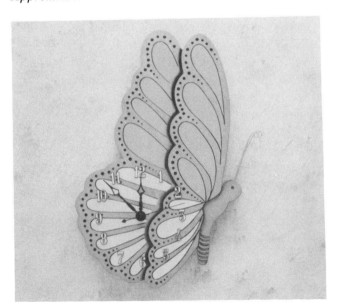

Alternate finish and special instructions

Drill two small holes in the top of the head, side by
side, for the antennas (two 6″ lengths of brass wire).
Using pointed pliers, turn one end of each wire in
a small circle. Insert the wire antennas in the holes
in the top of the head. Paint yellow on the commas
of the upper wings and orange on the lower. Paint
black finger dots around the outer edge of the
wings. Float black on the bottom side of the wood-
burned lines on the lower body (tail).

Turtle

⁵⁄₁₆" hole for clock shaft

Approximate dimensions: 9½" × 14". Scale: ½" = 1".

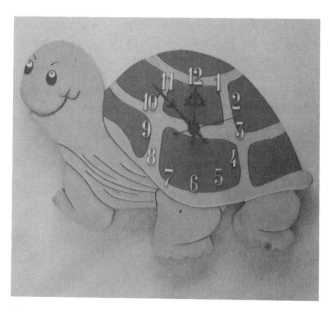

Alternate finish
Paint the lower part of the eyes black, and the upper part white, with a big black dot on the white. Paint the squares on the shell avocado green.

Frog

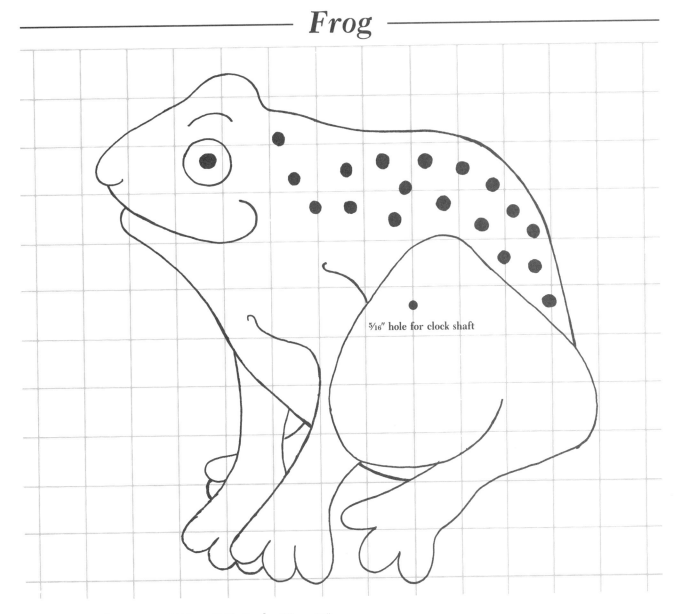

⁵⁄₁₆″ hole for clock shaft

Approximate dimensions: 9¼″ × 9¾″. Scale: ½″ = ⅞″.

Alternate finish

Do not wood-burn the inside of the eye nor the dots on the back. Sand lightly. Paint the outer part of the eye yellow with a big black dot in middle. Paint black spots on the back. Dry-brush a little yellow on the tummy.

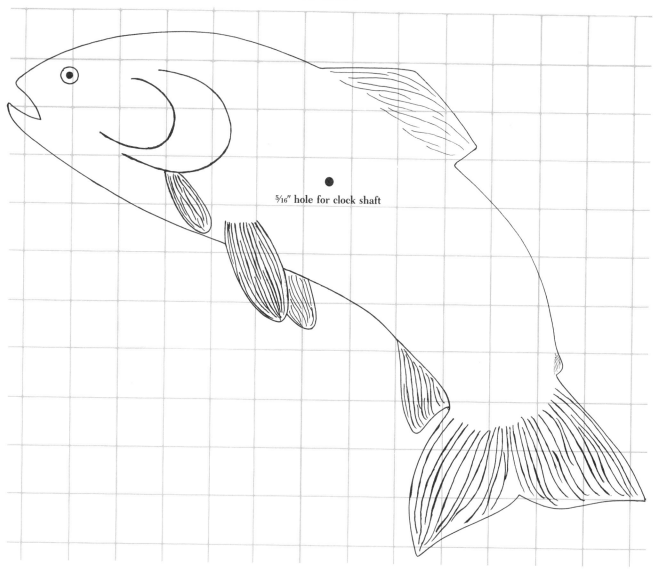

5/16" hole for clock shaft

Approximate dimensions: 10" × 19⅜". Scale: ½" = 1¼".

Alternate finish

Paint the eye yellow with a black middle. Dry-brush coral on the fins and through the middle of body.

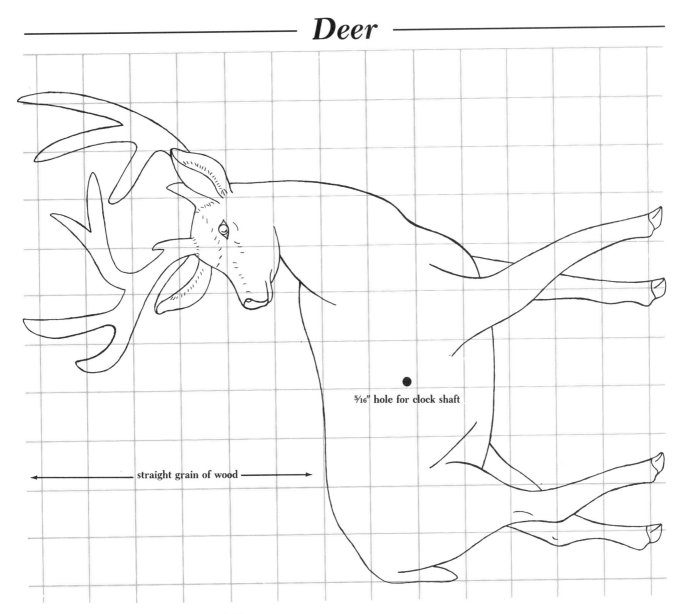

5/16″ hole for clock shaft

straight grain of wood

Approximate dimensions: 13⅛ × 17¼".
Scale: ½" = 1¼".

Alternate finish and special instructions
Note that the grain of the wood should run verti-
cally. Paint the middle of the eye black. Float
brown on the left side of the eyeball and white on
the right side. Paint the nose and the hooves black.
Put a small brown comma on the nose for a nostril.
Float tan on the inside of the ears.

sawtooth hangers

⁵⁄₁₆″ hole for clock shaft

Approximate dimensions: 10¾″ × 14″. Scale: ½″ = 1″.

Alternate finish and special instructions

This pattern uses two sawtooth hangers, one on the back of the head, one on the tail. Paint the middle of the eyes black. Float brown on the right side of the eyeballs and white on the left. Paint the nose black with a dark brown comma for a nostril. Float tan on the inside of the ears and the chest.

Squirrel

5/16" hole for clock shaft

Approximate dimensions: 10½" × 11½". Scale: ½" = 1".

Alternate finish

Paint the middle of the eye black. Float brown on the right side of the eyeball and white on the left. Paint the nose black with a dark brown comma for a nostril. Float tan on the inside of the ear, the underside of the body, and the underside of the tail; paint the large end of the acorn tan.

5/16" hole for clock shaft

Approximate dimensions: 8½" × 14". Scale: ½" = 1".

Alternate finish

Dry-brush pink on the inside of the ears. Paint the nose pink and the eyes brown. Float red on the tongue.

Piggy

⚫ 5/16" hole for clock shaft

Approximate dimensions: 10¼" × 11½". Scale: ½" = 1".

Alternate finish
Paint the eyeball black. Float brown on the right side of the eye and white on the left. Paint the hooves black; the nose pink; float white on the inside of the nostril on the right side, and coral on the left side; float pink on the inside of the ear.

Lamb

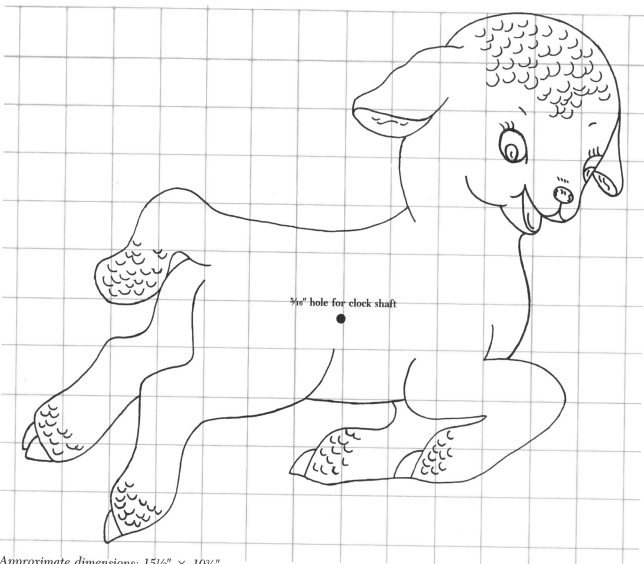

⁵⁄₁₆″ hole for clock shaft

Approximate dimensions: 15½″ × 10¾″.
Scale: ½″ = 1⅛″.

Alternate finish

Paint the eyes blue with black middles and small white commas. Paint the nose and the hooves black. Float red on the tongue. Load a No. 4 brush with grey and side-dip it in white. Make half circles or "C" strokes on the head, the tail, and the feet to look like wool. Float the inside of the ears with pink.

Hen

⁵⁄₁₆″ hole for clock shaft

Approximate dimensions: 10¼″ × 12½″. Scale: ½″ = 1″.

Alternate finish
Paint the eye black with a white dot; paint the beak and the feet straw; paint the comb red.

Rooter

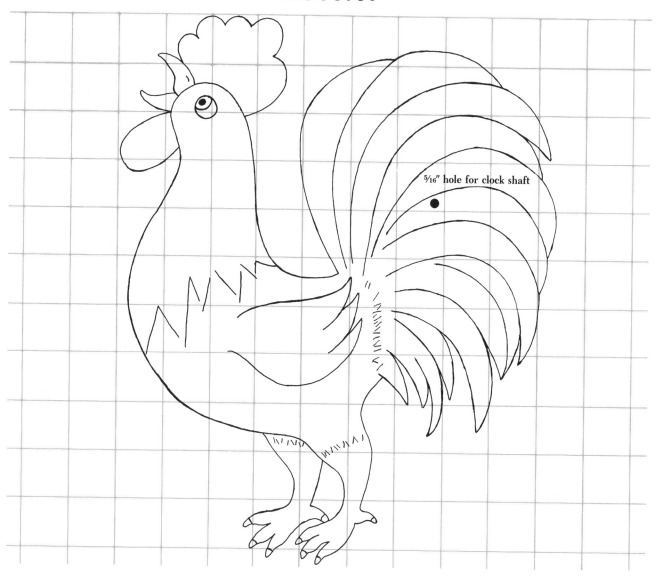

5/16" hole for clock shaft

Approximate dimensions: 10½" × 13". Scale: ½" = 1⅛".

Alternate finish

Do not wood-burn the inside of the eye. Paint the eye black with a large white dot; paint the comb red, the beak and the feet straw. The tail feathers may also be painted.

101 WOODEN CLOCK PATTERNS

Rooster on Grass

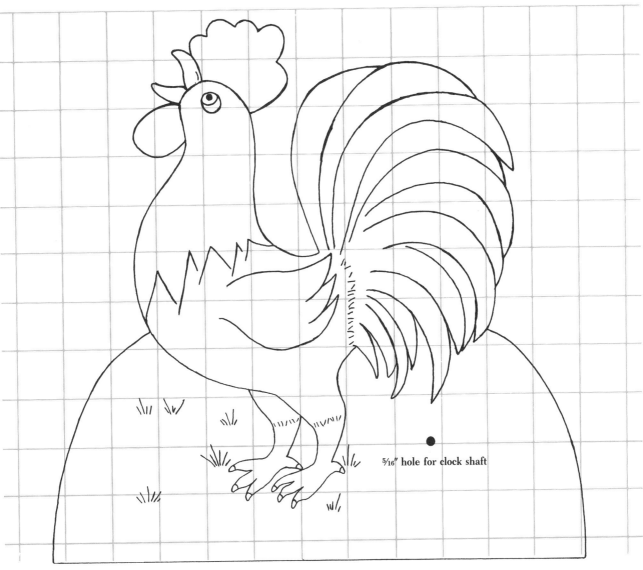

5/16" hole for clock shaft

Approximate dimensions: 10" × 10". Scale: 1/2" = 7/8".

Alternate finish

Do not wood-burn the inside of the eye. Paint the eye black with a large white dot; paint the beak and the feet straw; paint the comb red. The tail feathers may also be painted. Dry-brush green on the clumps of grass.

Dairy Cow

⁵⁄₁₆″ hole for clock shaft

Approximate dimensions: 10″ × 16½″. Scale: ½″ = 1¼″.

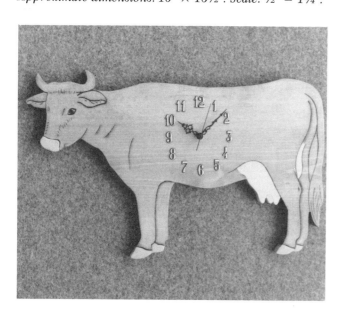

Alternate finish

Paint the middle of the eye black. Float brown on the left side of the eyeball and white on the right; paint the horns grey; paint the nose grey with a white comma for a nostril; paint the udder pink, the hooves grey. Float pink inside the ears.

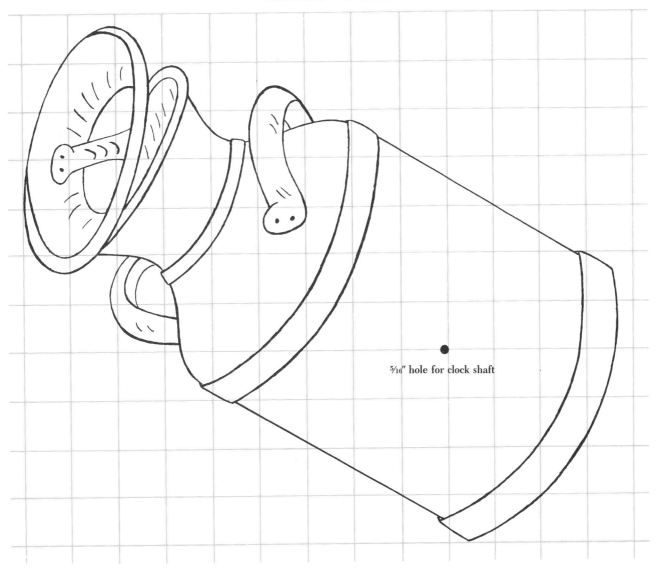

⁵⁄₁₆″ hole for clock shaft

Approximate dimensions: 6½″ × 13¾″. Scale: ½″ = 1″.

Alternate finish

Use any of three optional finishes. Paint strawberries or flowers of your choice around the clock. Paint or stencil a border on the rims around the milk can. Decals may be used around the middle or on the rims.

Bull

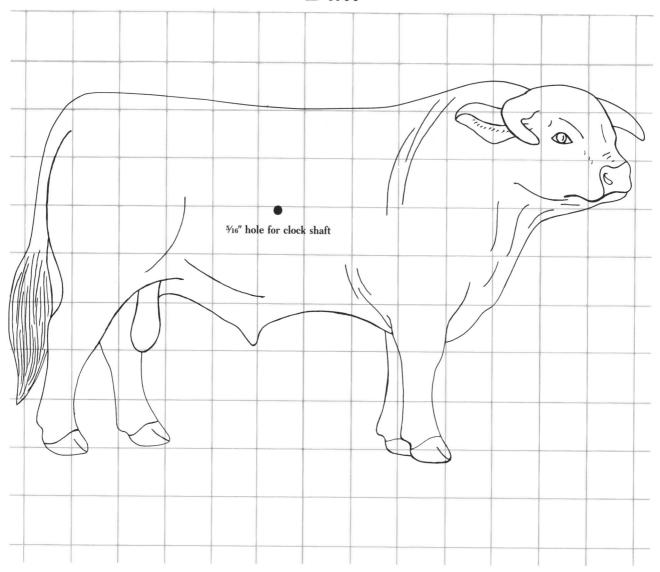

⁵⁄₁₆″ hole for clock shaft

Approximate dimensions: 10¼″ × 17″. Scale ½″ = 1¼″.

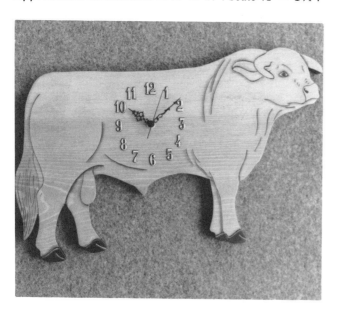

Alternate finish

Paint the middle of the eye black. Float brown on the right side of the eyeball and white on the left. Paint the horns and the hooves grey; paint the nose grey with a white comma for a nostril; float pink inside the ear.

Flying Eagle

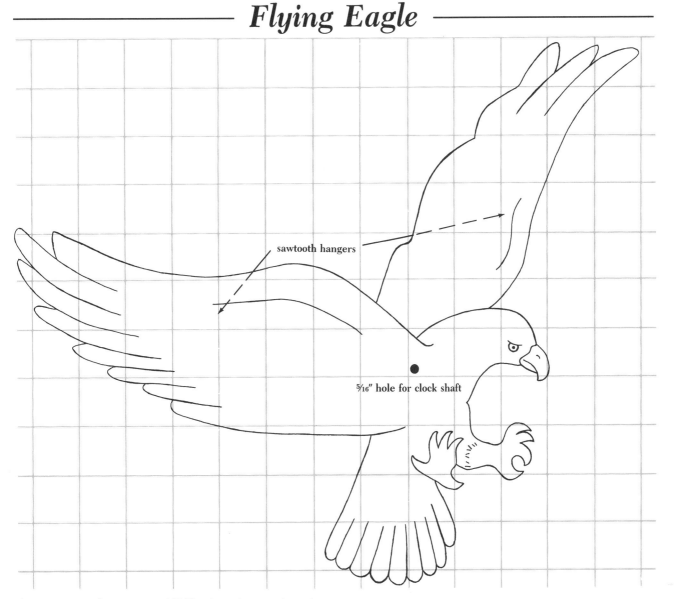

sawtooth hangers

⁵⁄₁₆″ hole for clock shaft

Approximate dimensions: 22¾″ wing tip to wing tip.
Scale: ½″ = 1⅝″.

Alternate finish
Paint the eye black with a white dot; paint the beak and the feet straw.

Swan

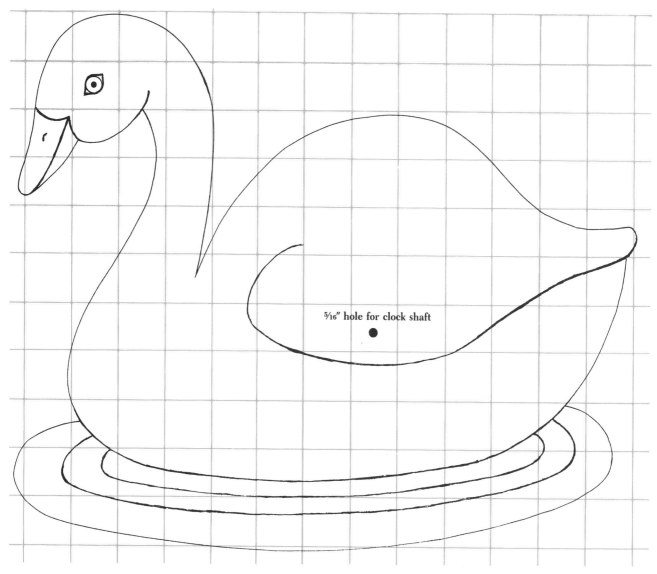

⁵⁄₁₆″ hole for clock shaft

Approximate dimensions: 12″ × 10″. Scale: ½″ = ⅞″.

Alternate finish

Do not wood-burn the water rings around the swan. Paint the outer eye light blue, the middle black with a white dot middle; paint the beak straw. Load a flat brush with light blue and side-tip it in white. Float ripples of water around the swan in white.

Goose with Bow

⁵⁄₁₆″ hole for clock shaft

Approximate dimensions: 8½″ × 14″. Scale: ½″ = 1″.

Alternate finish

Paint the eye black with a white comma and a dot. Paint the beak and the feet straw, and the bow medium blue.

Flying Duck

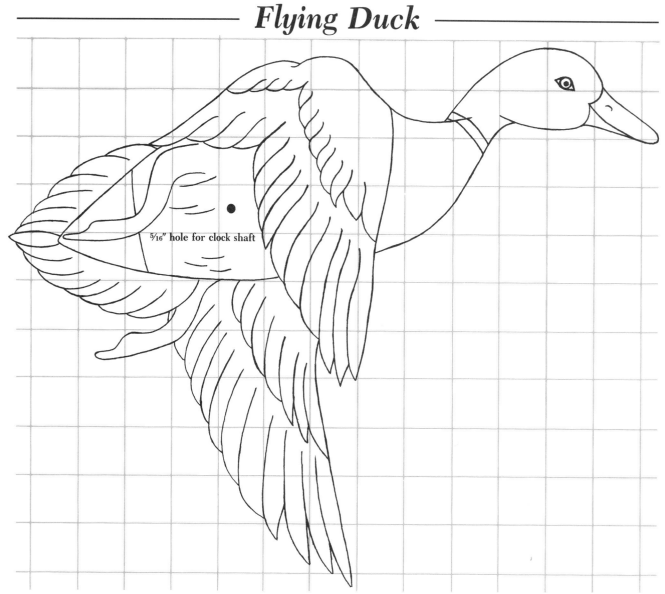

5/16" hole for clock shaft

Approximate dimensions: 18⅜" × 15¾".
Scale: ½" = 1½".

Alternate finish
Paint the head green, the ring around the neck, the beak, and the feet straw; paint the tip of the beak black; paint the eye yellow with a black center.

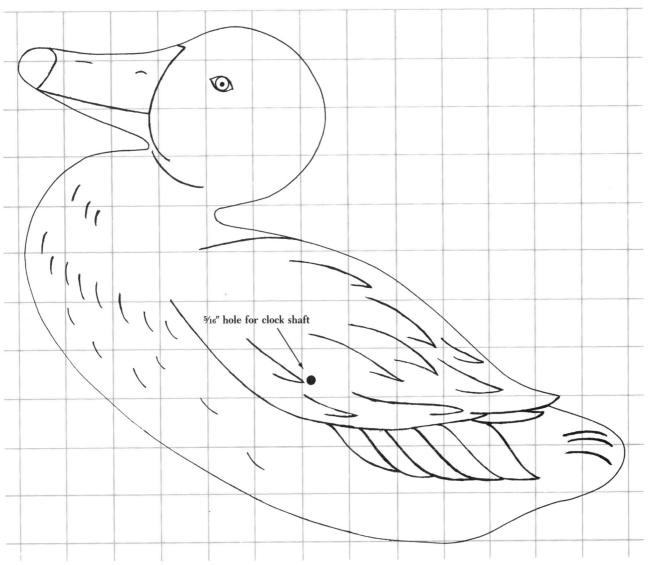

Approximate dimensions: 15½″ × 8½″. Scale: ½″ = 1″.

⁵⁄₁₆″ hole for clock shaft

Alternate finish

Paint the beak straw with a black tip; paint the eye yellow with a black middle.

Duck with Duckling

⁵⁄₁₆″ hole for clock shaft

Approximate dimensions: 10″ × 12″. Scale: ½″ = ⅞″.

Alternate finish
Paint the eyes black with a white comma and a dot. Paint the beaks, the straw and the duckling pale yellow. Shadow the beaks with gold and highlight them with ivory.

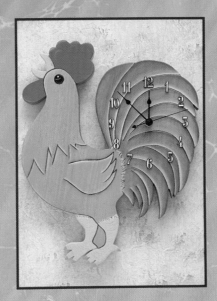

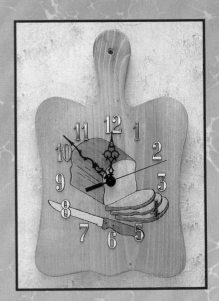

Top left: Butterfly (page 43) 9½″ × 14½″. Top middle: Rooster (page 54) 10½″ × 13″. Top right: Breadboard (page 114) 8½″ × 13½″. Above: Flying Duck (page 62) 18⅜″ × 15¾″. Left: Road Bike (page 96) 11¼″ × 16½″.

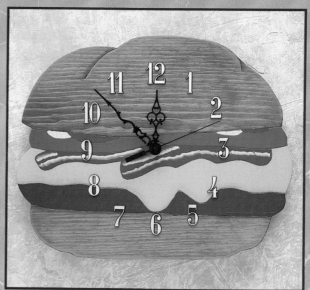

*Above: Apple (page 73) 8¼″ × 13¾″.
Top right: Mushroom (page 75)
11½″ × 12″. Middle right: Hamburger
(page 76) 11″ × 14″. Bottom right:
Cornucopia (page 71) 11½″ × 16¼″.*

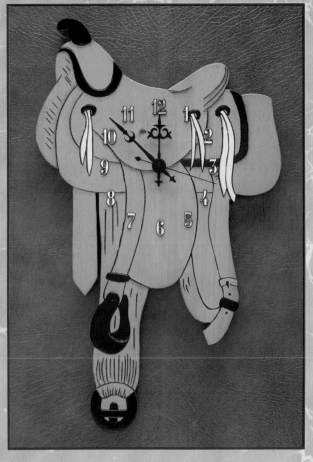

Top left: Puppy with Ball (page 33) 12¼″ × 10″. Middle left: Turtle (page 44) 9½″ × 14″. Bottom left: Owl on Log (page 67) 13½″ × 9″. Above: Saddle (page 24) 15¾″ × 10⅛″.

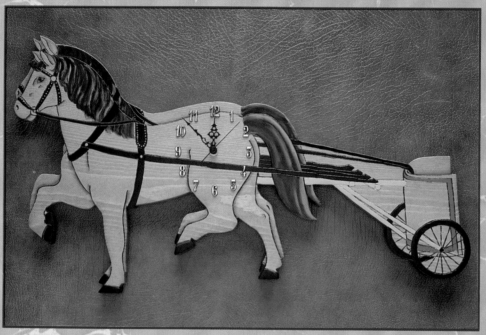

Top left: Baseball Mitt (page 81) 11″ × 11″. Top right: Poker Hand (page 110) 14⅝″ × 8¾″. Above: Chariot and Horses (page 23) 18⅛″ × 12¾″. Far right: Tiger (page 41) 13¾″ × 8¼″. Near right: Teddy Bear with Heart (page 39) 8½″ × 14″.

Penguin

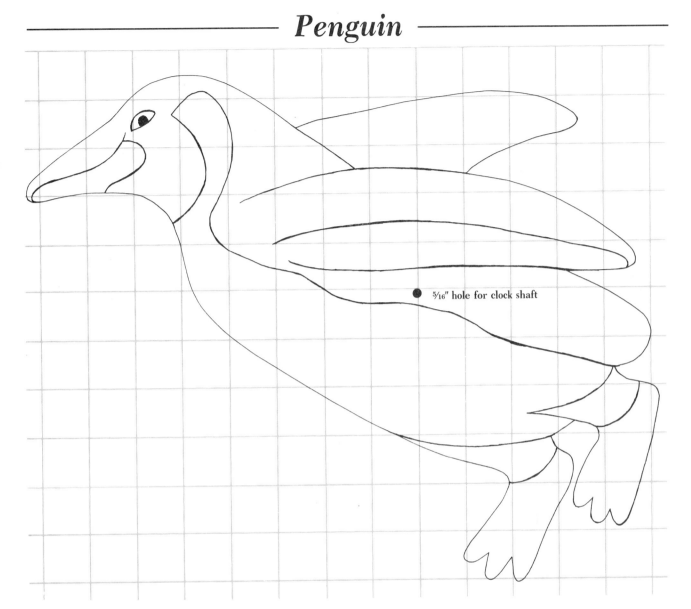

⁵⁄₁₆″ hole for clock shaft

Approximate dimensions: 9¾″ × 14″. Scale: ½″ = 1″.

Alternate finish

Paint the back, the top of the wings, and the legs black; paint the underside of the wings and the tummy white; paint the beak and the feet orange; paint the eye white with a black dot.

Owl on Branch

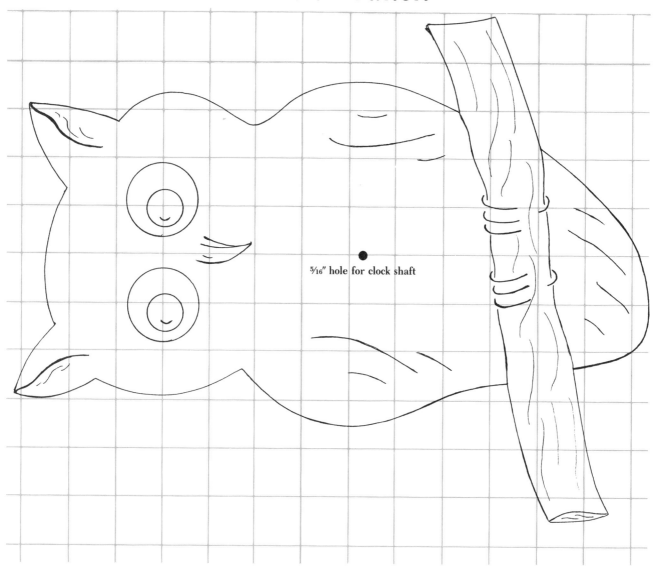

5/16" hole for clock shaft

Approximate dimensions: 10½" × 13½". Scale: ½" = 1".

Alternate finish
Paint the outside of the eyes and the beak yellow; paint the eyes black; float white on the right side of the eyeball; float tan on the inside of the ears.

Owl on Log

5/16" hole for clock shaft

Approximate dimensions: 13½" × 9". Scale: ½" = 1".

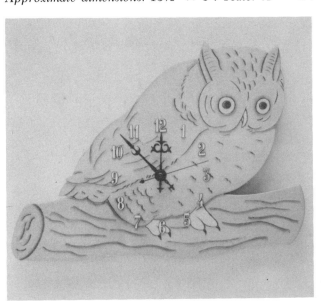

Alternate finish
Paint the outer eye yellow and the middle black; paint the beak and the feet straw; float tan on the underside of the body and the inside of the ears.

Rose

⁵⁄₁₆″ hole for clock shaft

Approximate dimensions: 14¼″ × 10″. Scale: ½″ = 1″.

Alternate finish
Paint the rose yellow and the leaves green.

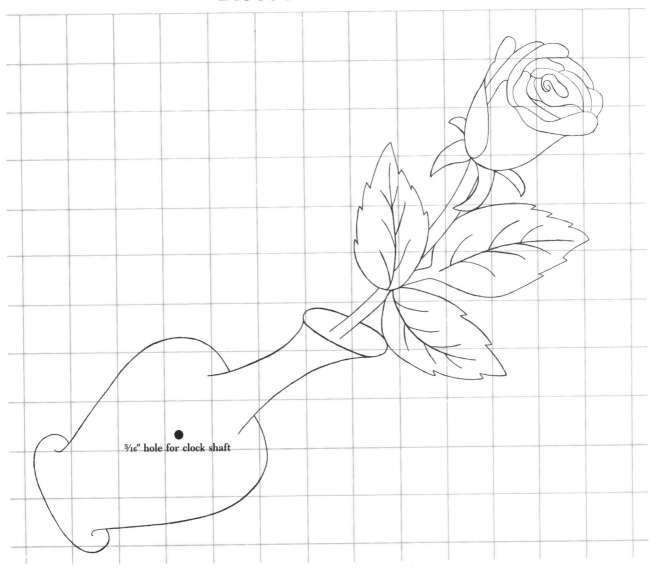

⁵⁄₁₆″ hole for clock shaft

Approximate dimensions: 9″ × 21¾″. Scale: ½″ = 1½″.

Alternate finish

Paint the rose pink or yellow; paint the sepal, the stem, and the leaves green. The vase may be painted the color of your choice.

Rosebud on Card

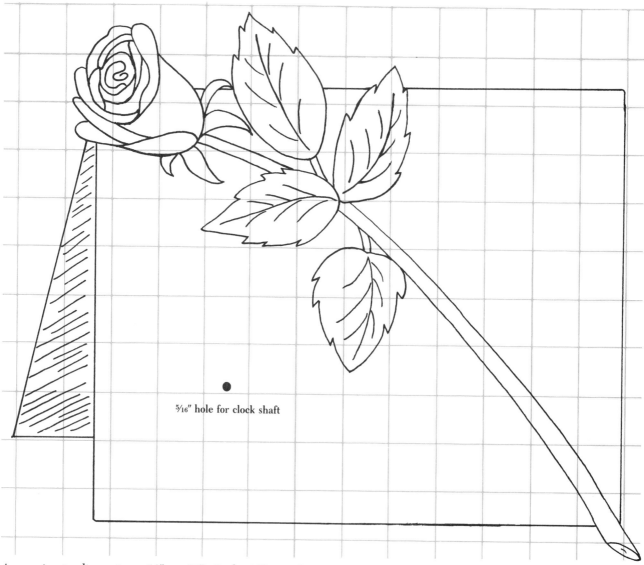

Approximate dimensions: 10″ × 12″. Scale: ½″ = ⅞″.

5/16″ hole for clock shaft

Alternate finish
Paint the rose pink or yellow; paint the sepal, the stem, and the leaves green.

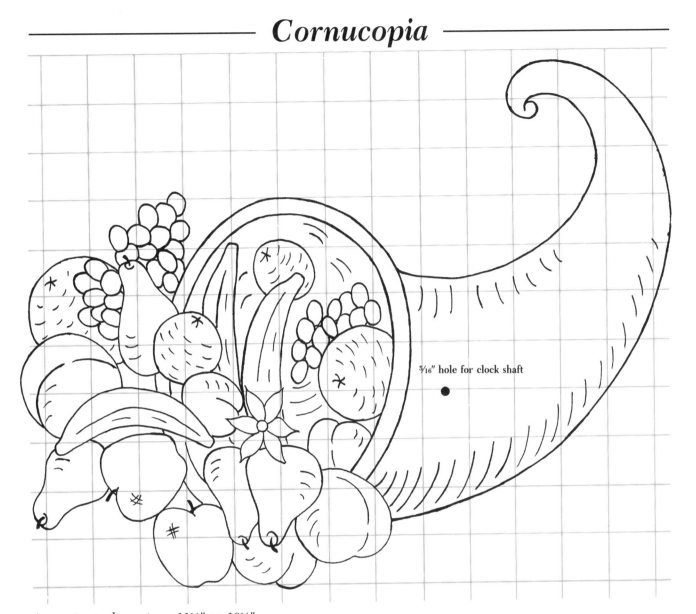

⁵⁄₁₆″ hole for clock shaft

Approximate dimensions: 11½″ × 16¼″.
Scale: ½″ = 1⅛″.

Alternate finish
Paint the flower white with a yellow middle; paint the fruit their own natural colors.

Strawberry

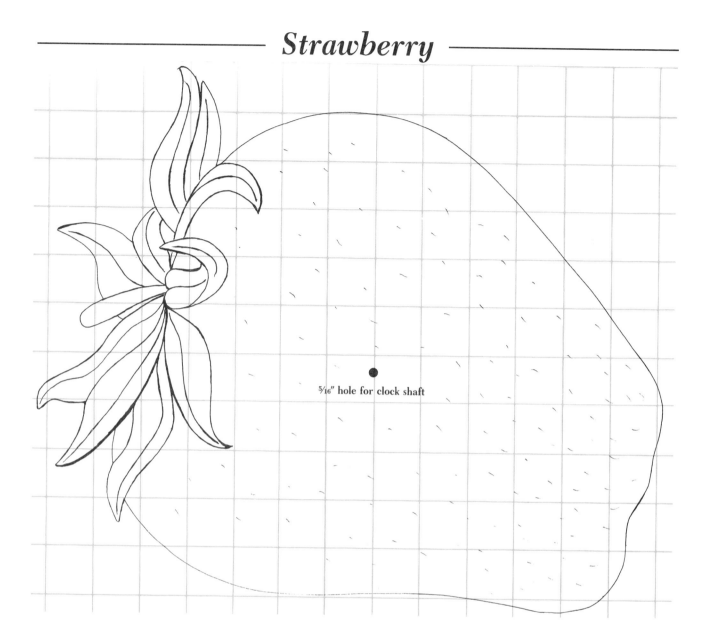

⁵⁄₁₆″ hole for clock shaft

Approximate dimensions: 10¼″ × 14″. Scale: ½″ = 1″.

Alternate finish
Do not wood-burn the seeds on the strawberry.
Paint the berry red, the leaves green, and the seeds
straw.

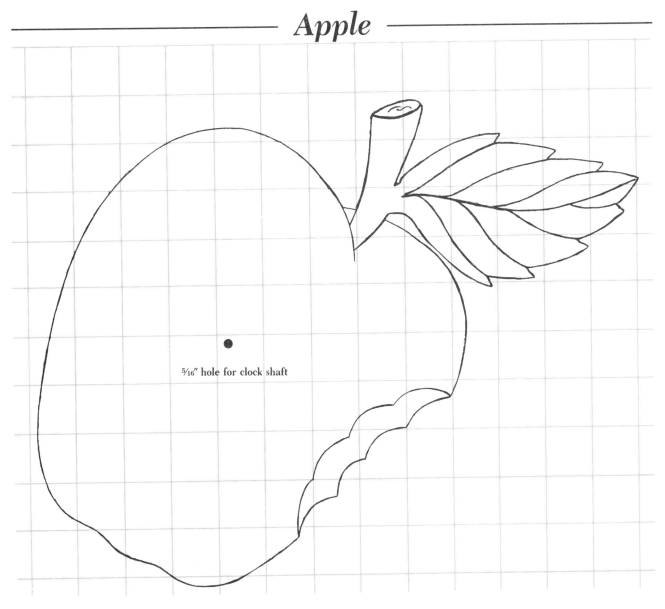

⁵⁄₁₆" hole for clock shaft

Approximate dimensions: 8¼" × 13¾". Scale: ½" = 1".

Alternate finish

Paint the apple red, the leaf green, and the stem brown. Paint the "bite" portion antique white.

Idaho Potatoes

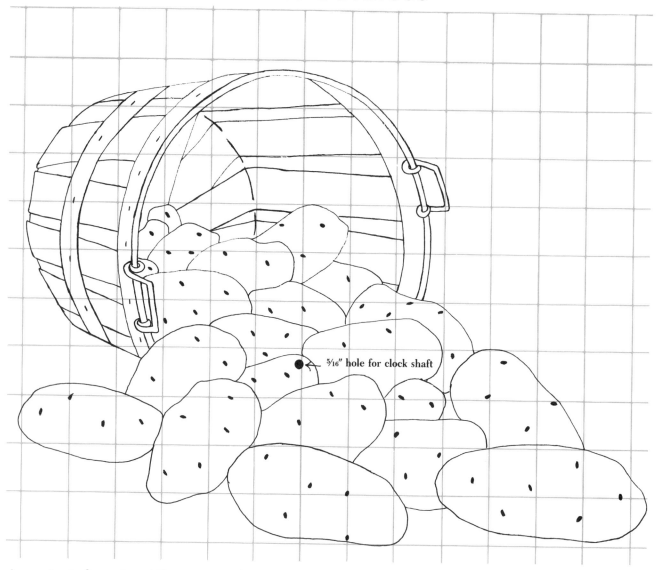

⁵⁄₁₆″ hole for clock shaft

Approximate dimensions: 11″ × 16¼″. Scale: ½″ = 1⅛″.

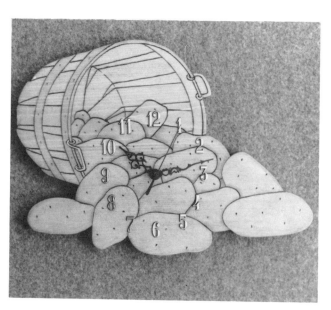

Alternate finish
Paint the handles grey and the rims around the basket medium blue or turquoise.

101 WOODEN CLOCK PATTERNS

Mushroom

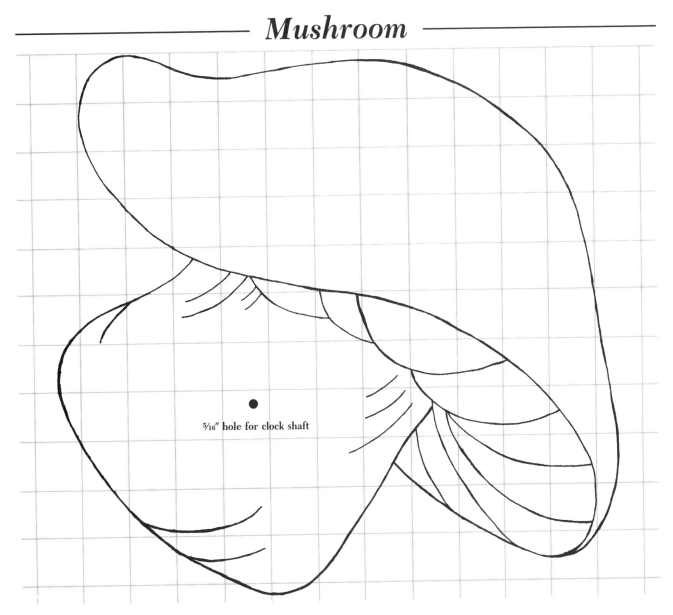

⁵⁄₁₆″ hole for clock shaft

Approximate dimensions: 11½″ × 12″. Scale: ½″ = 1″.

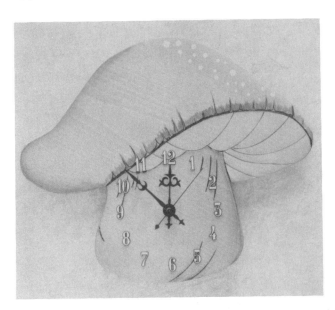

Alternate finish

Do not stain. Seal the wood. Paint the upper part of the mushroom bright yellow; paint the underpart of the mushroom and the stem ivory. Fill a No. 8 brush with ivory and side-tip it in dark brown, then side-load one side of the stem. Fill a brush with bright yellow and side-tip it in red iron oxide and then side-load one side of the upper parts, and on the other side fill a brush with bright yellow and side-tip it in ivory. Put some dots randomly along one side.

Hamburger

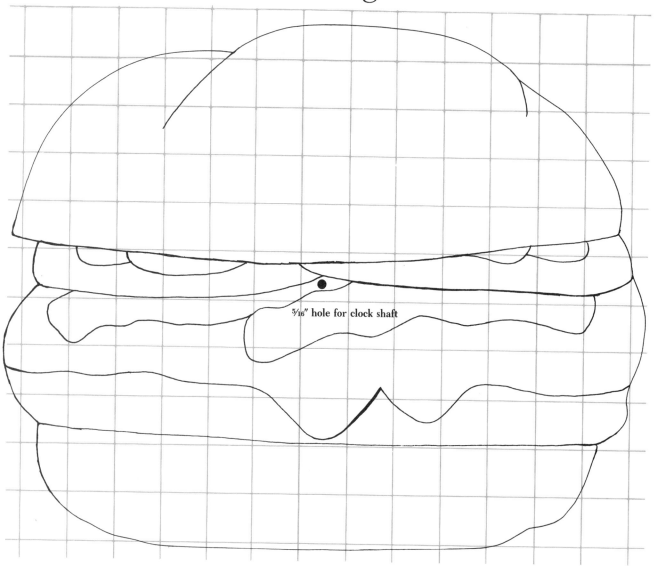

5/16" hole for clock shaft

Approximate dimensions: 11" × 14". Scale: ½" = 1".

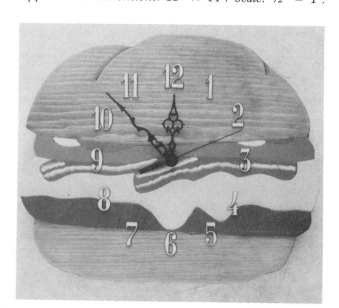

Alternate finish
Paint the onion antique white; paint the tomato bright red; paint the cheese deep yellow; paint the bacon burnt sienna.

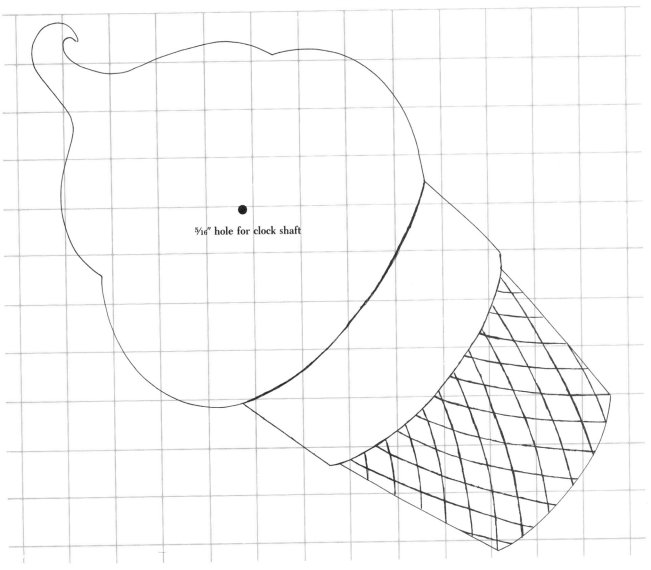

5⁄16″ hole for clock shaft

Approximate dimensions: 9″ × 14″. Scale: ½″ = 1″.

Alternate finish
Paint the ice cream antique white or pink.

Basketball Player

5⁄16″ hole for clock shaft

Approximate dimensions: 10″ × 17½″. Scale: ½″ = 1″.

Alternate finish

Paint the outer part of the eye white with blue dots for the eyeballs and a tiny black dot in the middle of the blue for the pupil. Float brown around the outer edge of the eye, the nose, and the lips. Paint the shirt, the shorts, the socks, and the shoes orange.

Skier on Sun

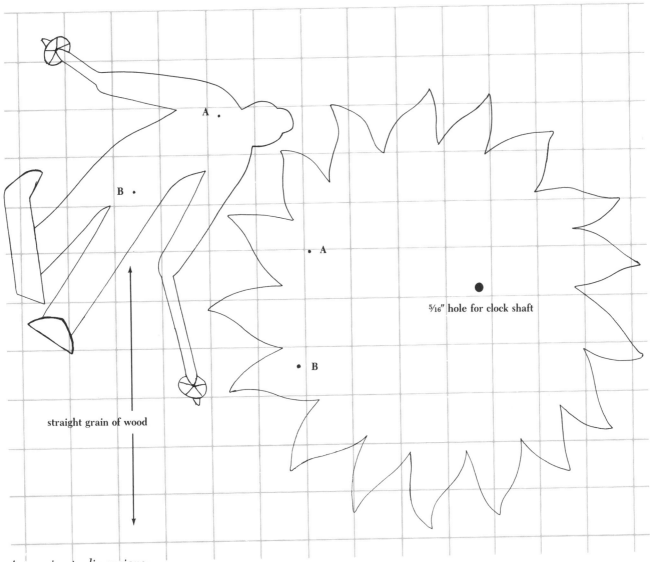

A •

B •

• A

• B

● 5/16″ hole for clock shaft

straight grain of wood ↕

Approximate dimensions:
Sun should measure 11½″ tip-to-tip. Scale: ½″ = 1″.

Special instructions

Note the direction of the wood grain as indicated on the pattern. Drill 2 small screw holes through A and B on the sun and about ⅜″ deep on the back side of the skier. Trace the detailed pattern lightly on the top side of the skier cutout and wood-burn it with the "hot tool." Sand with a fine-grit sandpaper after wood-burning and before staining. Stain the skier using a darker stain, stain the sun using a lighter stain. Seal and varnish. After the varnish is dry, assemble the skier to the sun using screws.

Alternate finish

Rout a 3″ hole on the back side of the sun ½″ deep and use the multicolor clock face instead of the numbers.

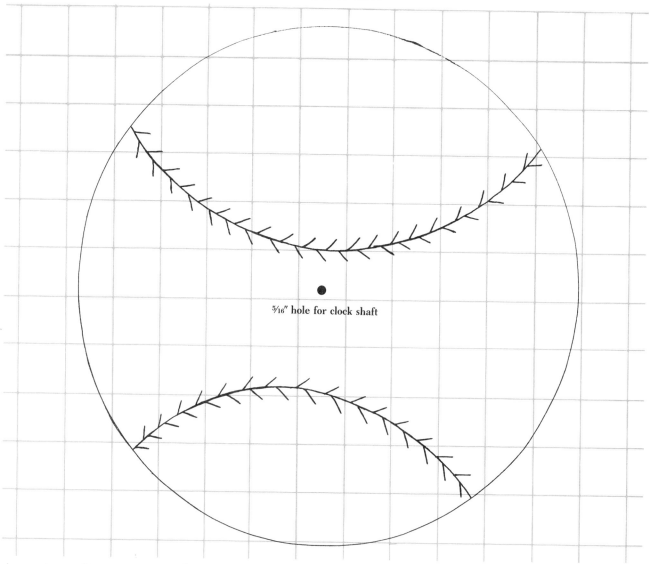

5/16" hole for clock shaft

Approximate dimensions: 10¾" diameter.
Scale: ½" = 1".

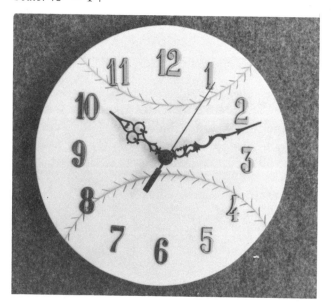

Alternate finish

Apply 3 coats of white paint with a sponge brush. Trace the pattern lightly on the wood piece. Use a liner brush to paint the sew lines grey and the stitching red.

Baseball and Mitt

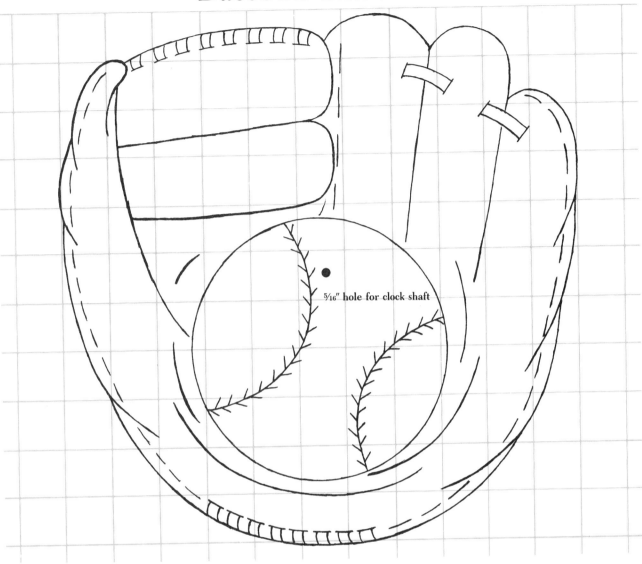

5/16" hole for clock shaft

Approximate dimensions: 11" × 11". Scale: ½" = 1".

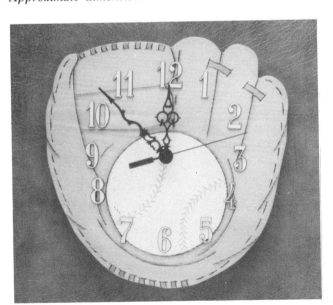

Alternate finish
Wood-burn all but the stitching on the ball. Paint the ball white; paint the seam grey; paint the stitching red.

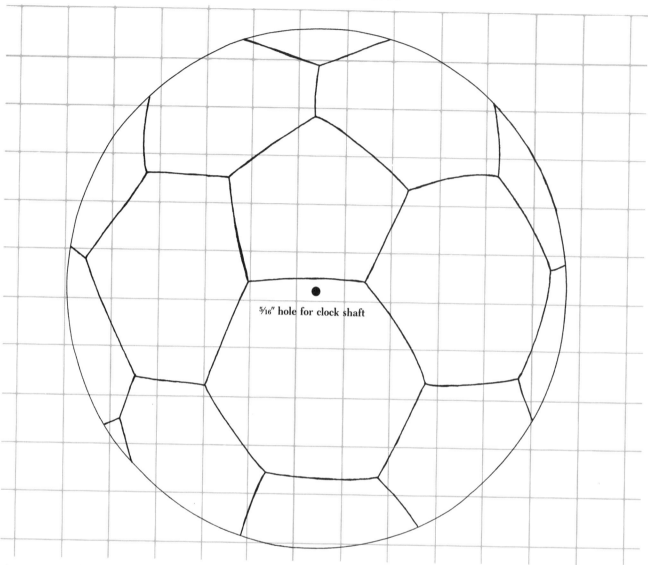

⁵⁄₁₆″ hole for clock shaft

Approximate dimensions: 10¾″ diameter.
Scale: ½″ = 1″.

Alternate finish

Paint 3 coats of white with a 2″ sponge brush. Trace the pattern on and draw lines using a liner brush and black paint. Paint the appropriate sections black.

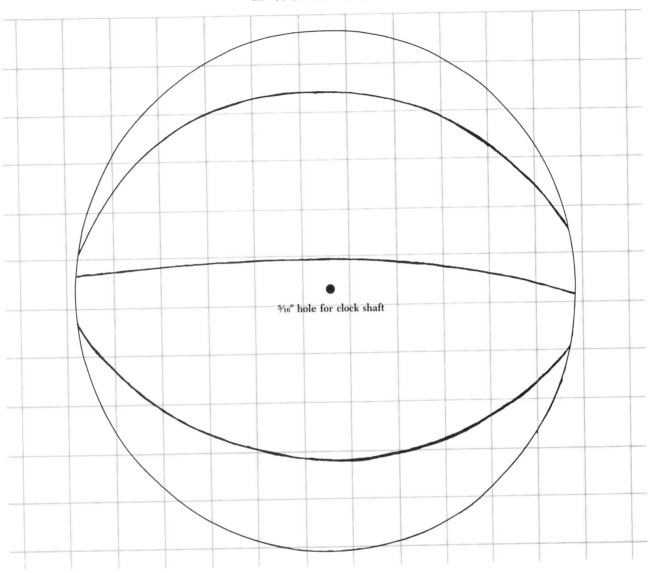

5/16″ hole for clock shaft

Approximate dimensions: 10¾″ diameter.
Scale: ½″ = 1″.

Alternate finish
Rout the 3″ hole ½″ deep. Use a basketball player multicolor clock face instead of numbers.

Football

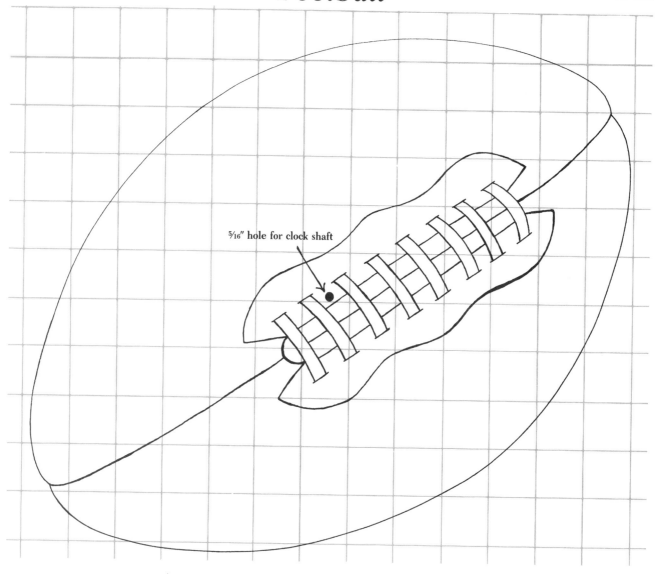

⁵⁄₁₆″ hole for clock shaft

Approximate dimensions: 9½″ × 13¼″. Scale: ½″ = 1″.

Alternate finish
Paint the laces white.

Football Helmet

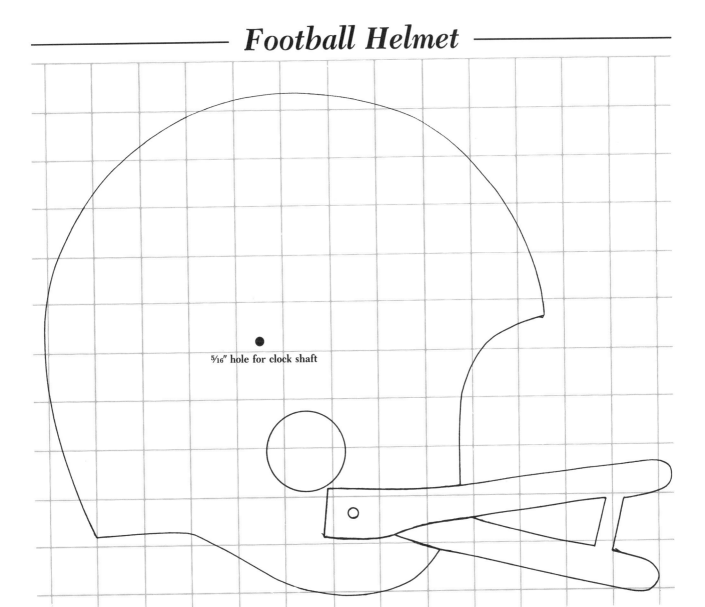

⁵⁄₁₆″ hole for clock shaft

Approximate dimensions: 13½″ × 10½″. Scale: ½″ = 1″.

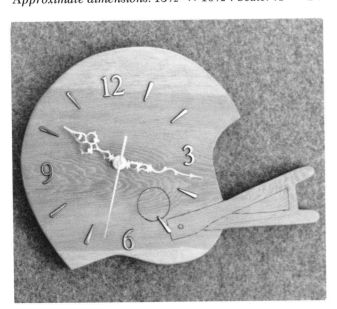

Alternate finish
Use either of two finishes. Paint the face guard grey. Your favorite team emblem may be applied. Or, rout the 3″ hole ½″ deep and use the football multicolor clock face in place of the numbers.

Bowling Pin and Ball

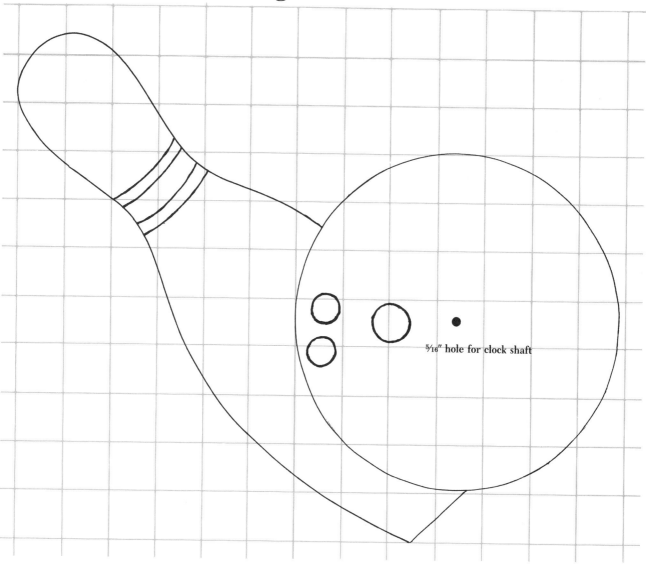

⁵⁄₁₆″ hole for clock shaft

Approximate dimensions: 8½″ × 13¼″. Scale: ½″ = 1″.

Alternate finish
Paint the pin white; paint the stripes red; paint the ball the color of your choice; paint the finger holes black.

Bowling Ball and Three Pins

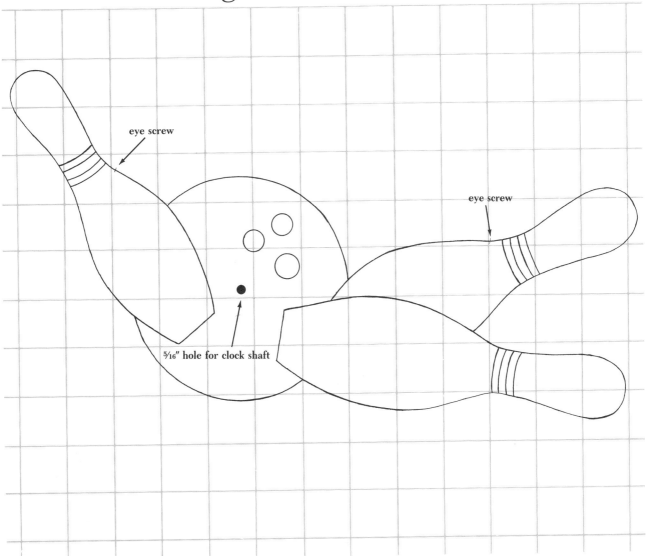

eye screw

eye screw

⁵⁄₁₆" hole for clock shaft

Approximate dimensions: 9⅜" × 21⅜".
Scale: ½" = 1½".

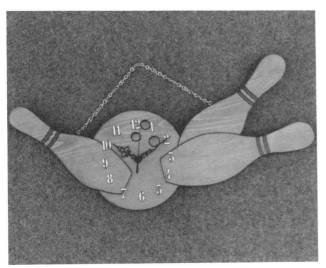

Special instructions

After varnishing or painting, screw in the eye screws as per the pattern and attach a gold-tone chain hanger.

Alternate finish

Paint the pins with 3 coats of white paint and paint the ball the color of your choice. Paint the finger holes black. Paint red stripes around the necks of the pins.

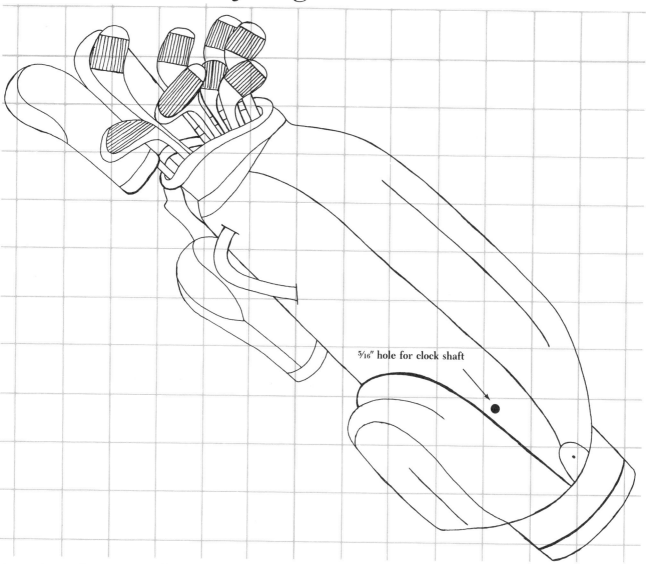

⁵⁄₁₆″ hole for clock shaft

Approximate dimensions: 6⅞″ × 17½″.
Scale: ½″ = 1¼″.

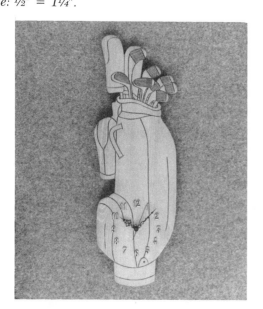

Alternate finish
Paint the socks and the bag the colors of your choice.

⁵⁄₁₆″ hole for clock shaft

Approximate dimensions: 6⅛″ × 13⅛″. Scale: ½″ = ⅞″.

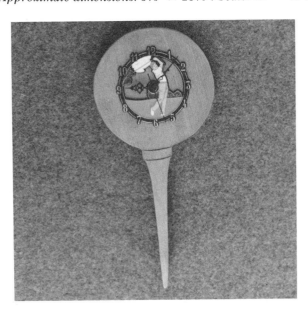

Alternate finish
Use either of two alternate finishes. Paint the ball white; paint the tee the color of your choice. Or, rout the 3″ hole ½″ deep and use a multicolor clock face.

Tennis Racquet with Ball

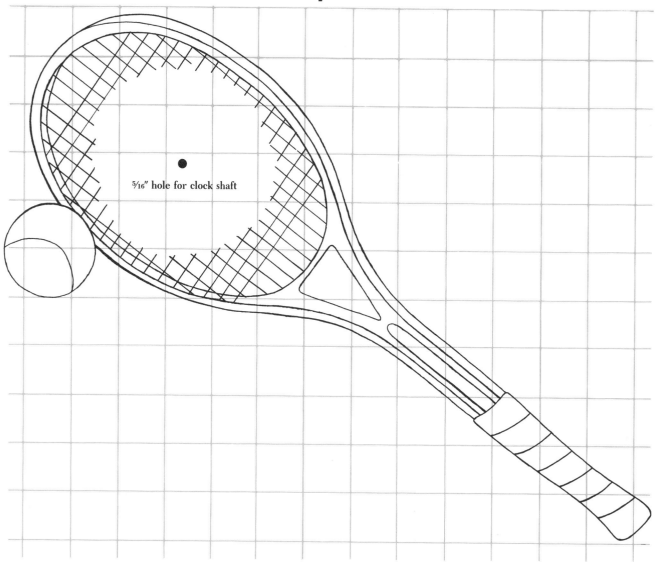

⁵⁄₁₆″ hole for clock shaft

Approximate dimensions: 8⅛″ × 20″. Scale: ½″ = 1¼″.

Alternate finish

Paint the handle black; paint the ball the color of your choice. The multicolor tennis clock face may be used in place of numbers. If so, rout the 3″ hole ½″ deep.

Snowmobile

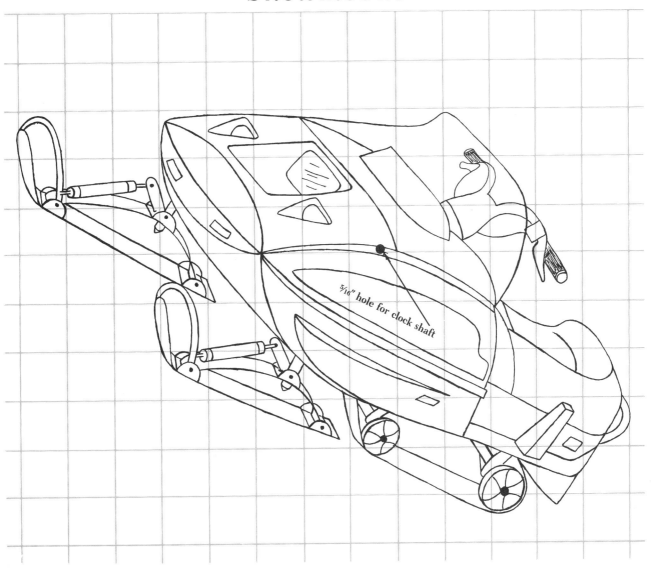

5/16" hole for clock shaft

Approximate dimensions: 8¾" × 16¼".

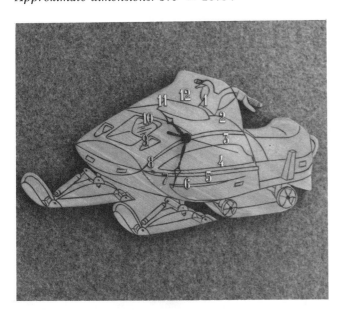

Alternate finish

Paint the skis grey; paint the seat and the track black; the machine may be left as is or it may be painted the color of your choice. If you paint the whole machine, do not stain it; seal the wood instead.

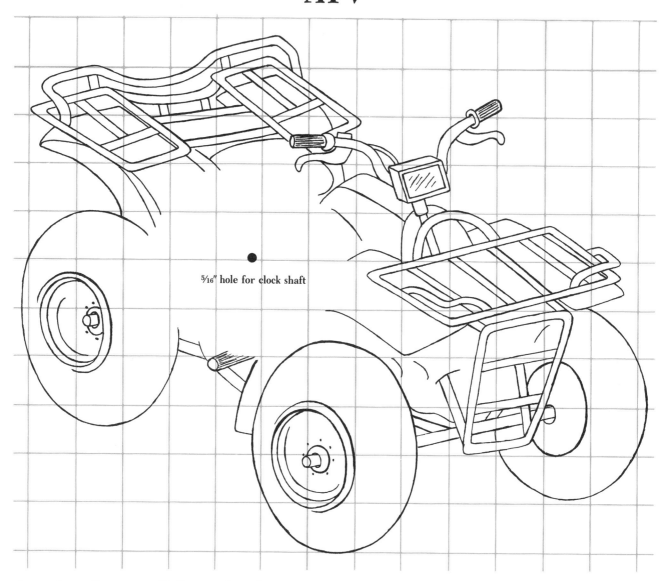

⁵⁄₁₆″ hole for clock shaft

Approximate dimensions: 13¾″ × 10¾″. Scale: ½″ = 1″.

Alternate finish

Paint the tires and the bars black. If you prefer, the racks and the handle bars could be painted silver or grey.

Airplane on Cloud

⁵⁄₁₆″ hole for clock shaft

Approximate dimensions: 10½″ × 16¼″.
Scale: ½″ = 1⅛″.

Alternate finish

Paint the engines grey. Side-load a No. 6 brush with white and float the inside circle of the clouds. The plane may also be painted.

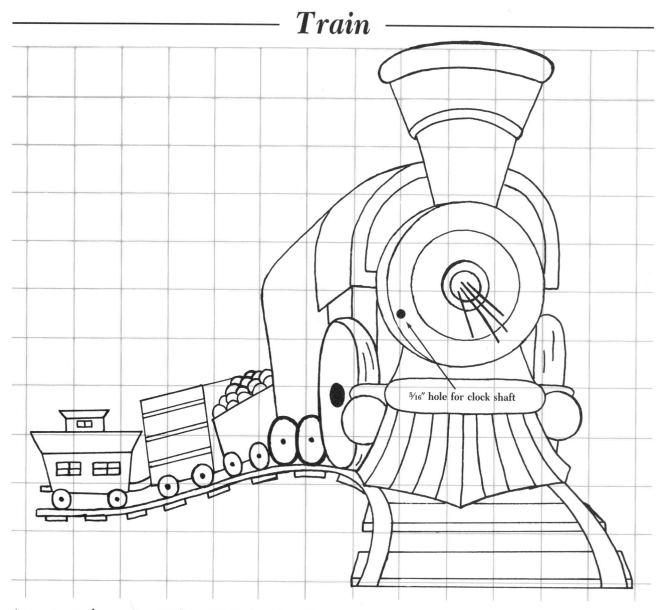

5/16" hole for clock shaft

Approximate dimensions: 11½" × 13". Scale: ½" = 1".

Alternate finish

Paint the wheels black; paint the coal black; paint the headlight and the windows in the caboose yellow; paint the stripes on the boxcar red; paint the tracks grey.

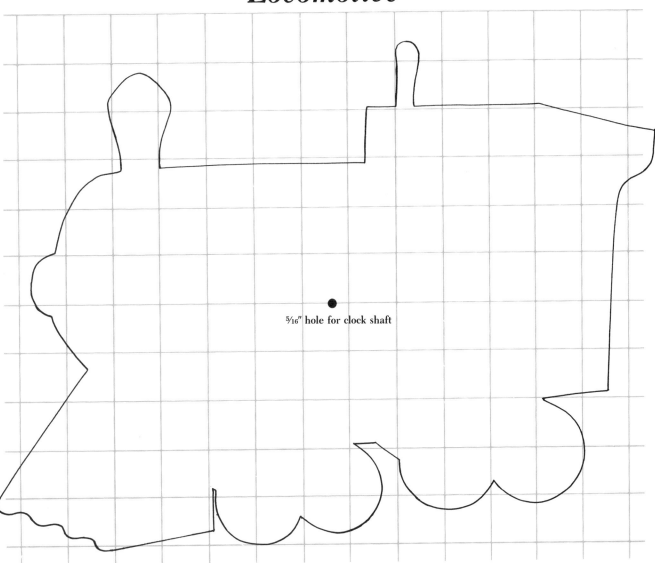

⁵/₁₆″ hole for clock shaft

Approximate dimensions: 14″ × 10½″. Scale: ½″ = 1″.

Alternate finish

Rout the 3″ hole ½″ deep. Use the train multicolor clock face in place of numbers.

Road Bike

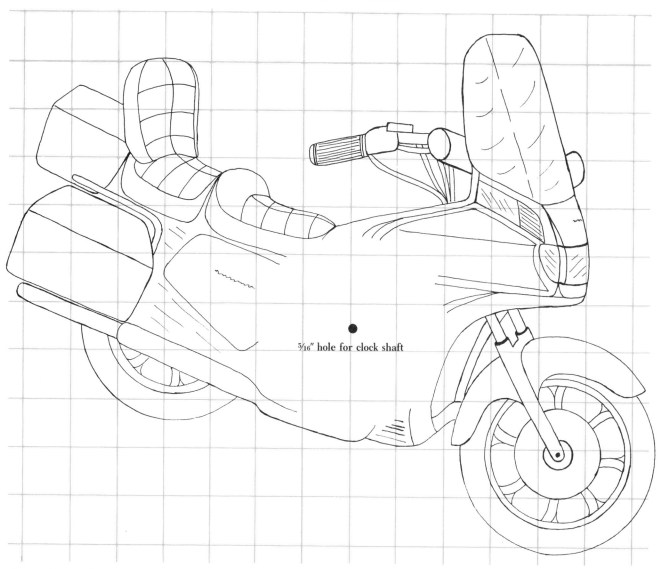

5/16″ hole for clock shaft

Approximate dimensions: 11¼″ × 16½″.
Scale: ½″ = 1⅛″.

Alternate finish
Paint the tires and the seat black; paint the saddle bags maroon; paint the headlight yellow; paint the spokes, pipes, and fender either grey or silver.

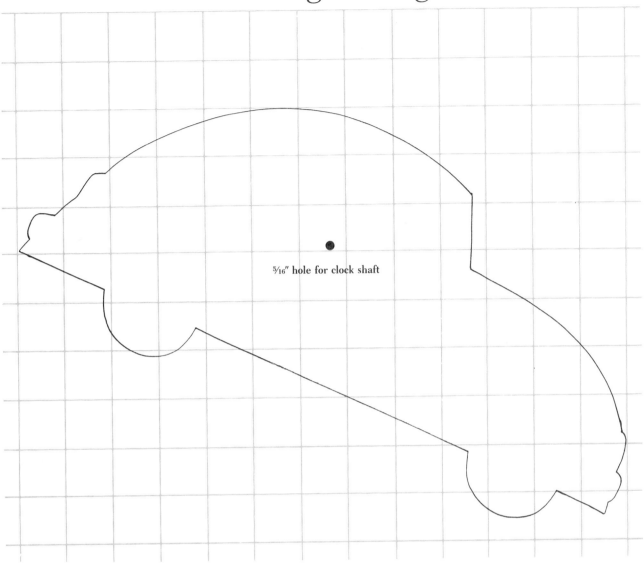

⁵⁄₁₆″ hole for clock shaft

Approximate dimensions: 14″ × 6½″. Scale: ½″ = 1″.

Alternate finish

Rout the 3″ hole ½″ deep. Use the "racing flags" multicolor clock face in place of numbers. "Herby," "Love Bug," or a number could be painted, stenciled, or wood-burned on the car.

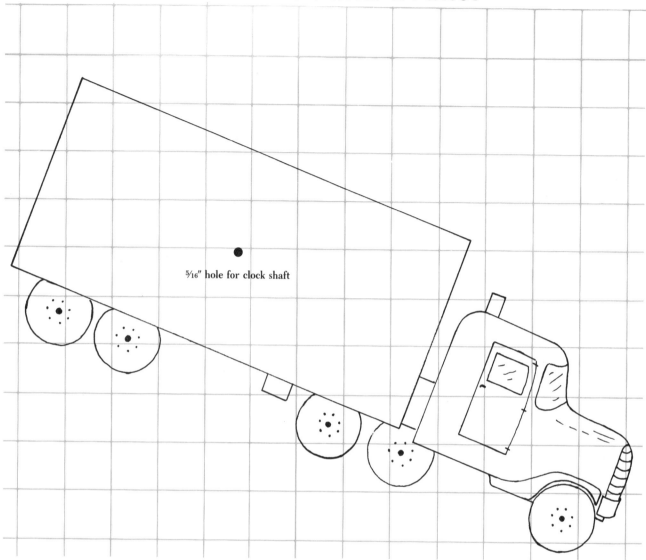

5/16" hole for clock shaft

Approximate dimensions: 6¼" × 15¾".
Scale: ½" = 1⅛".

Alternate finish
Paint the grille, the bumper, and the smokestack either grey or silver. Rout the 3" hole ½" deep. Use the truck multicolor clock face in place of the numbers. A name may be painted or stencilled on the trailer and/or on the door of the cab.

Fifth-Wheel Truck

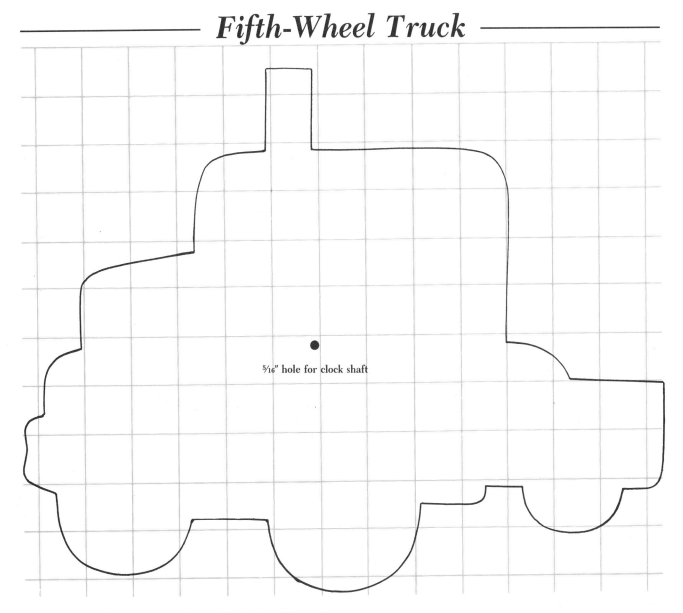

5/16" hole for clock shaft

Approximate dimensions: 14" × 11". Scale: ½" = 1".

Alternate finish
Rout the 3" hole ½" deep. Use the truck multicolor clock face in place of the numbers.

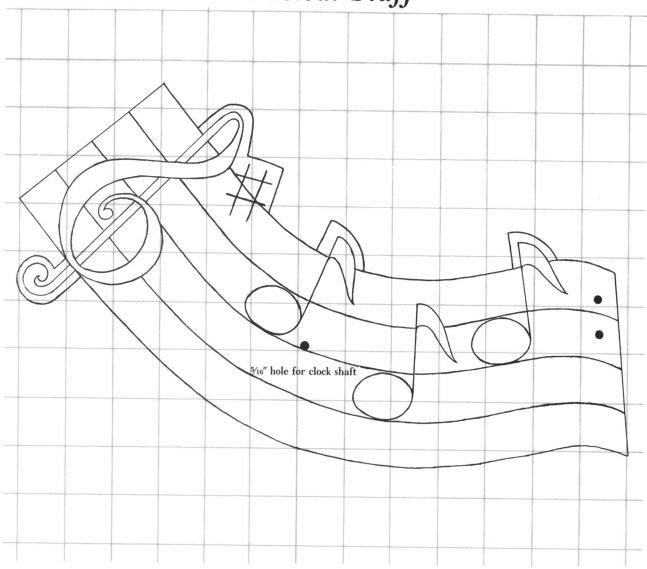

Approximate dimensions: 12¾" × 21". Scale: ½" = 1½".

Alternate finish
Paint the notes and the treble clef black.

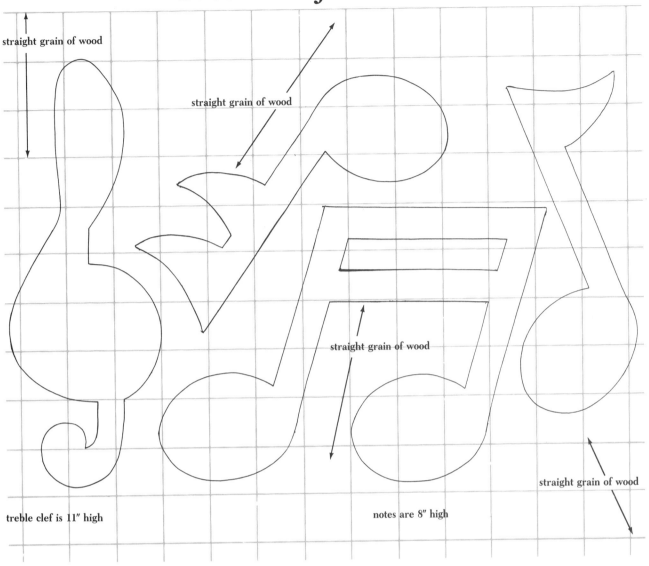

straight grain of wood

straight grain of wood

straight grain of wood

straight grain of wood

treble clef is 11" high

notes are 8" high

Approximate dimensions: Notes: 8" high.

Alternate finish and special instructions

These are plaques only. Follow the grain of the wood as noted on the pattern. Paint the notes and the treble clef black. Each piece uses one sawtooth hanger. These plaques can be arranged around or above one of the musical instruments.

Grand Piano

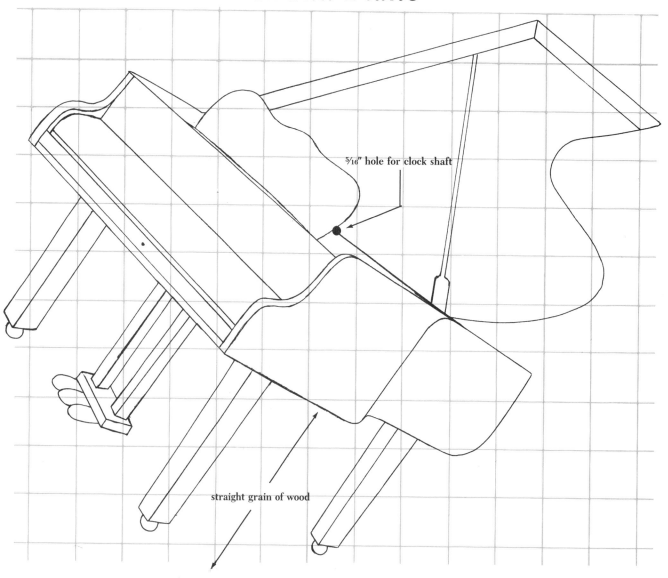

⁵⁄₁₆″ hole for clock shaft

straight grain of wood

Approximate dimensions: 12″ × 13¾″. Scale: ½″ = 1″.

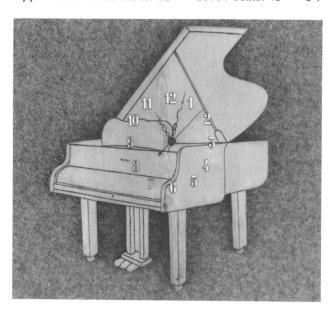

Special instructions

Follow the grain of the wood as noted on the pattern. Finish without the clock and use it as a wall decoration, along with the notes and the treble clef (p. 101).

Violin

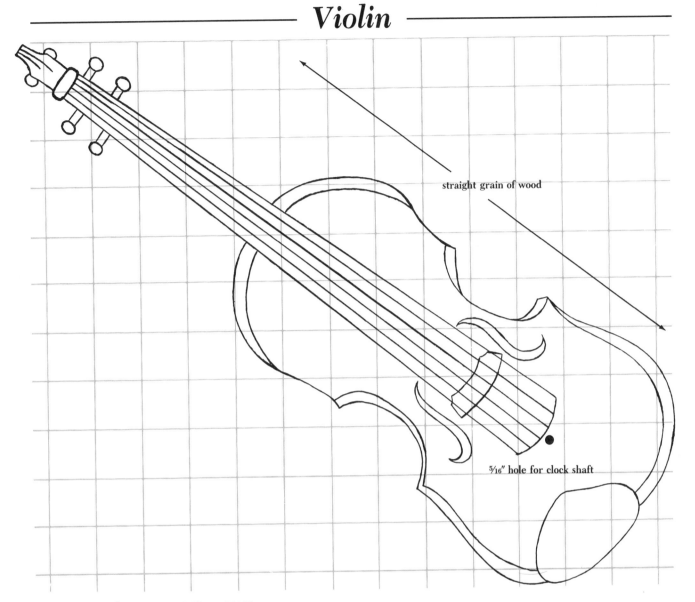

straight grain of wood

⁵⁄₁₆" hole for clock shaft

Approximate dimensions: 6¼" × 16⅞".
Scale: ½" = 1⅛".

Alternate finish and special instructions
Follow the grain of the wood as noted on the pattern. Paint the chin pad black. This piece can be used with or without a clock.

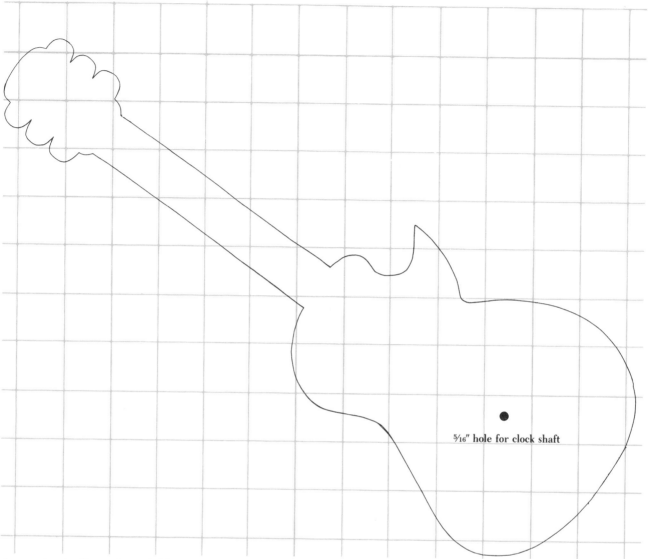

5⁄16″ hole for clock shaft

Approximate dimensions: 6½″ × 18¾″.
Scale: ½″ = 1¼″.

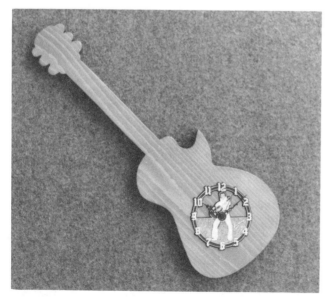

Alternate finish
Rout the 3″ hole ½″ deep. Use a musical theme multicolor clock face in place of the numbers.

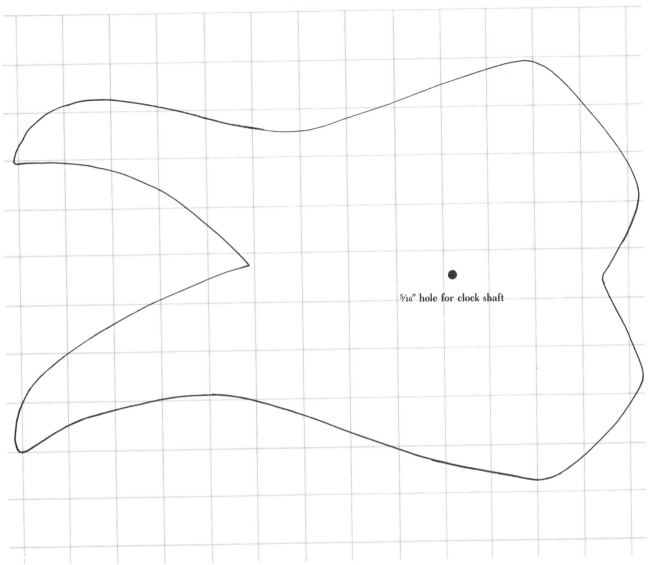

⁵⁄₁₆″ hole for clock shaft

Approximate dimensions: 9¼″ × 15½″.
Scale: ½″ = 1⅛″.

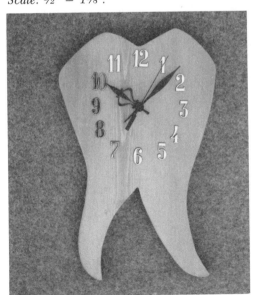

Alternate finish
Do not stain. Seal the wood and paint with antique white.

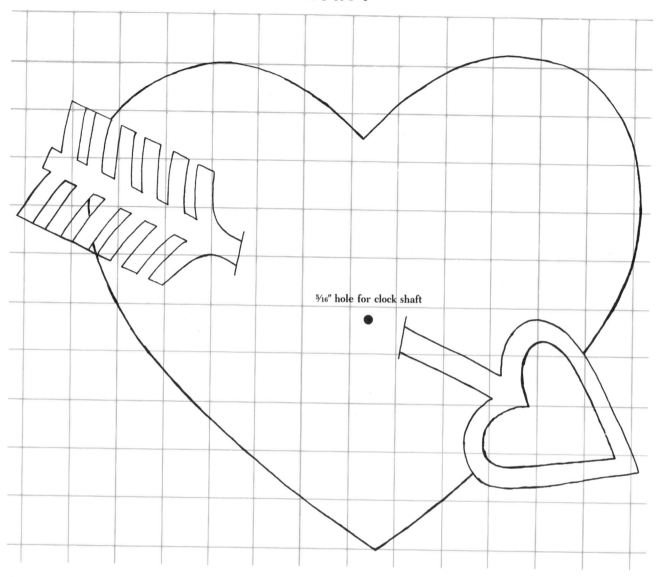

5/16" hole for clock shaft

Approximate dimensions: 10¼" × 15½". Scale: ½" = 1".

Alternate finish
Paint the arrow red; a photo may be découpaged on.

Anchor and Ship Wheel

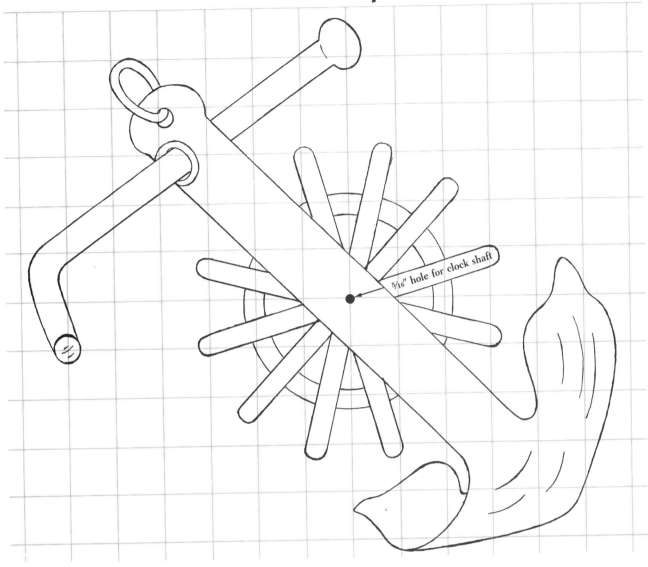

5/16" hole for clock shaft

Approximate dimensions: 11½" 15½". Scale: ½" = 1".

Alternate finish
Paint the anchor grey.

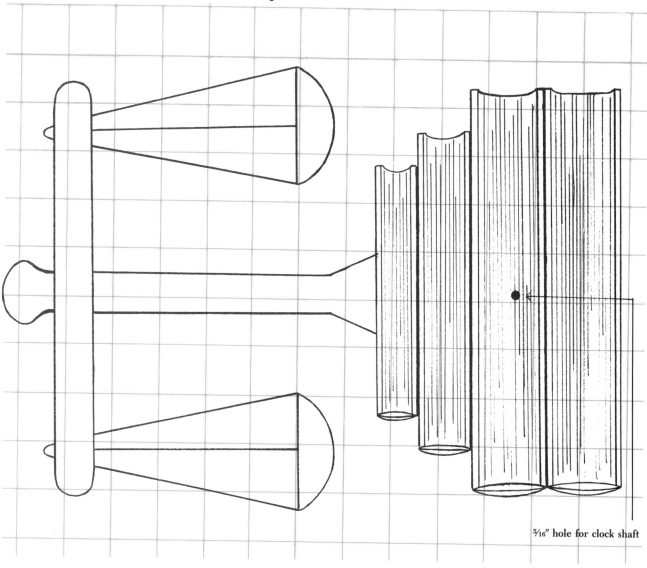

Approximate dimensions: 9¼" × 13½". Scale: ½" = 1".

⁵⁄₁₆" hole for clock shaft

Alternate finish

Paint the scales grey and the pages of the books antique white.

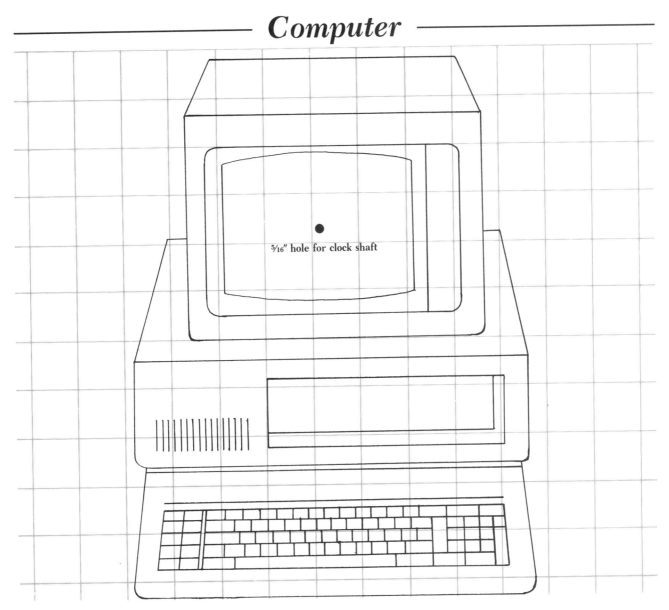

5/16" hole for clock shaft

Approximate dimensions: 9½" × 12⅜".
Scale: ½" = 1⅛".

Alternate finish
Paint the screen and the keyboard grey.

5/16″ hole for clock shaft

Approximate dimensions: 14⅝″ × 8¾″.
Scale: ½″ = 1⅛″.

Alternate finish
Paint the diamonds red and the spades black. The cards may be painted white.

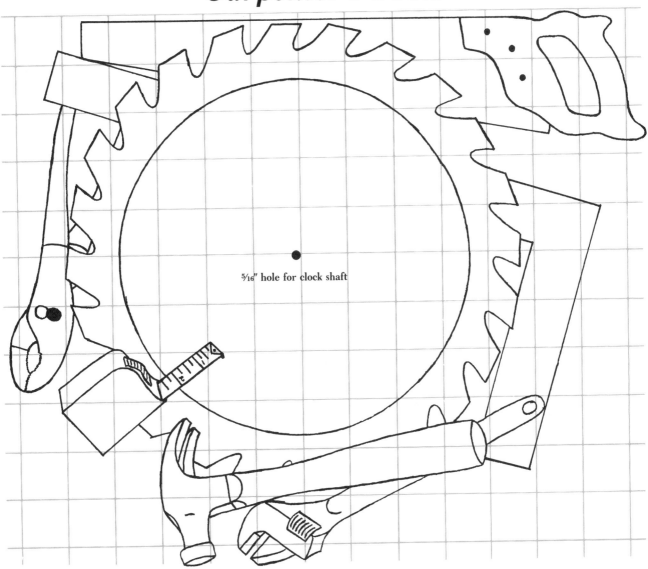

5/16" hole for clock shaft

Approximate dimensions: 11½" × 13½". Scale: ½" = 1".

Alternate finish

Paint the handsaw blade, the hammerhead, the crescent wrench and the pliers grey; paint the handle of the pliers red; paint the tape yellow.

Praying Hands

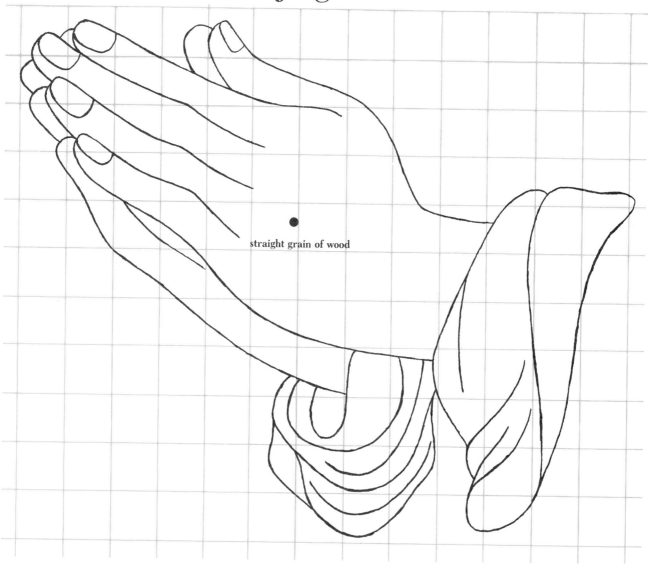

straight grain of wood

Approximate dimensions: 10″ × 14″. Scale: ½″ = 1″.

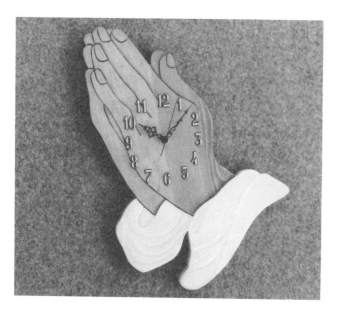

Alternate finish
Rout the 3″ hole ½″ deep. Use any religious theme multicolor clock face instead of the numbers.

Open Book

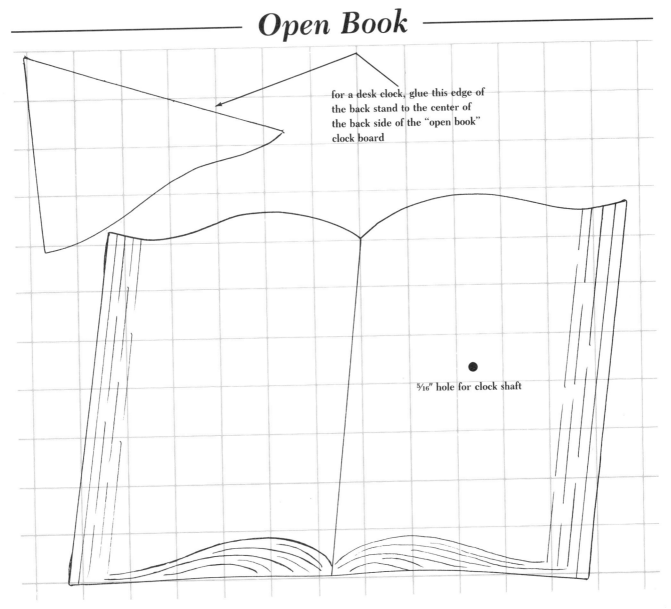

for a desk clock, glue this edge of the back stand to the center of the back side of the "open book" clock board

⁵⁄₁₆" hole for clock shaft

Approximate dimensions: 7" × 10¼". Scale: ½" = ⅞".

Special instructions
Wood-burn a verse on the left side of the book. Glue the stand to the back as per the pattern (for a desk clock). Nail the sawtooth hanger on the back in the spot where the clock balances itself (for a wall clock).

Alternate finish
Paint the edges of the book gold; paint or stencil the verse gold or black. A verse may be applied with découpage instead of painted.

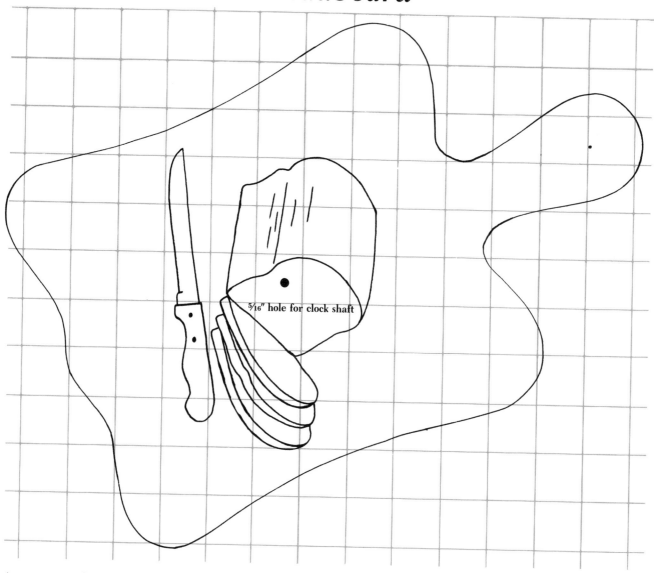

Approximate dimensions: 8½″ × 13½″. Scale: ½″ = 1″.

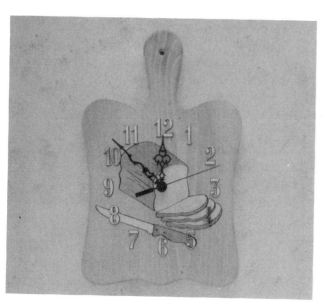

Alternate finish

Paint the knife blade grey; paint the handle black; paint the inside of the loaf of bread and the slices of bread antique white.

Commode

5/16″ hole for clock shaft

Approximate dimensions: 8½″ × 14″. Scale: ½″ = 1″.

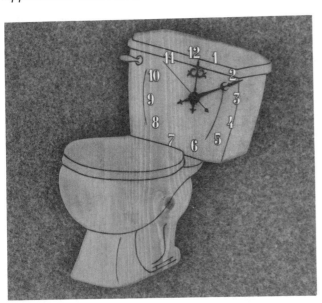

Alternate finish

Paint this clock to match your bathroom, either with flowers, or with a skunk on it; or wood-burn and stain it with flowers painted or stencilled on. Decals may also be used.

Duck Coatrack

Approximate dimensions: 17½″ × 11¼″.
Scale: ½″ = 1¼″.

Special instructions

Drill three ½″ holes ⅝″ deep; drill two ¼″ holes through at each end, for wall mounting. With a ½″ bit, drill over the top of these two holes just deep enough so that the plugs will fit in and cover the screw heads. Sand thoroughly with the grain of wood. Trace the detailed pattern lightly on the top side of the cutout and wood-burn with the "hot tool." Sand with a fine grit sandpaper after wood-burning, and before staining. Stain, seal, and varnish. Finish the Shaker pegs and insert them in the holes.

Alternate finish

Follow the instructions above through stain and seal. Sand lightly. Paint the beak straw with a black tip; paint the eye yellow with a black center. Apply two coats of varnish. Finish the Shaker pegs and insert them in the holes.

Unicorn Necklace Holder

Approximate dimensions: 13¼" × 10½". Scale: ½" = 1".

Special instructions
Finish the five tie holder pegs and insert them in the holes. Nail two sawtooth hangers on the back.

Alternate finish
Paint the middle of the eye black with a small white comma; paint the unicorn white. Fill a No. 6 flat brush with grey paint. Placing the chisel edge of the brush at the base of the mane, pull outward to the ends of the mane. Do the same with the tail, starting at the body. Paint the hooves black and the horn antique white.

Musical Staff Coffee Mug Holder

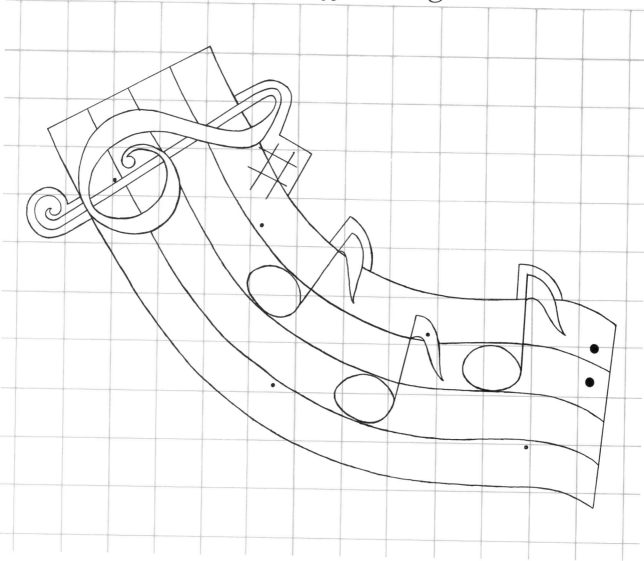

Approximate dimensions: 21" × 9⅜". Scale: ½" = 1½".

Special instructions

Drill five ½" holes ⅝" deep for the mug pegs. Nail sawtooth hangers on the back, one on each end.

Alternate finish

Paint the notes and the treble clef black.

— Kitten Note (or Calendar) Pad Holder —

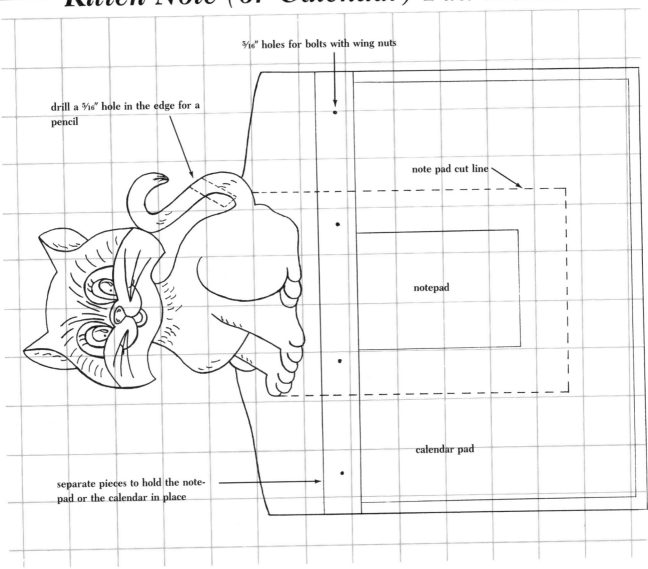

⁵⁄₁₆″ holes for bolts with wing nuts

drill a ⁵⁄₁₆″ hole in the edge for a pencil

note pad cut line

notepad

calendar pad

separate pieces to hold the note-pad or the calendar in place

Approximate dimensions: Calendar Pad: 12¾″ × 18¼″.
Note Pad: 6½″ × 16¼″. Scale: ½″ = 1⅜″.

Special instructions

Use the small size pattern for the notepad holder and the large size pattern for the calendar pad holder. Trace the outline of the pattern on the lumber and saw out the shape. Drill ⁵⁄₁₆″ holes through the two designated spots (on both the main wood piece and on the strip) for the bolts. On the note-pad holder, drill a ⁵⁄₁₆″ hole for the pencil.

Alternate finish

Paint the middle part of the eye black. Paint a white comma on the left side and a dot on the lower right side. Paint the nose black with tiny white commas for the nostrils. Float the inside of the ears with pink or tan.

Cuddly Teddy Bear Puzzle

Approximate dimensions: 11¼" × 14¼". Scale: ½" = 1".

Special instructions

Trace an outline of the pattern on the lumber and saw out the shape. Sand thoroughly with the grain of the wood. Trace the detailed pattern (of the teddy bear, not the puzzle lines) lightly on the top side of the cutout and wood-burn with the "hot tool." Trace the puzzle lines lightly and saw into puzzle pieces. Sand with a fine-grit sandpaper. Stain, seal, and varnish.

Alternate finish

Paint the eyes black with white commas on the right sides of the eyes and a dot on the lower left sides; paint the muzzle cream and the nose black with small white commas for nostrils; float red on the mouth; dry-brush the cream color inside the ears and on the paws.

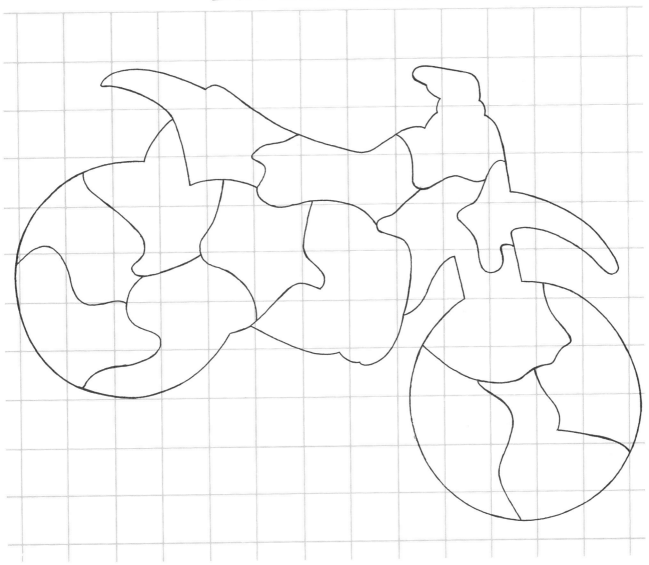

Approximate dimensions: 14" × 10½". Scale: ½" = 1".

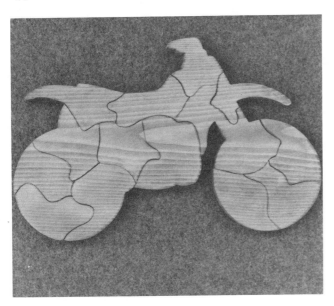

Special instructions

Trace the complete pattern on the lumber and saw out the shape and the puzzle pieces. Sand thoroughly with the grain of the wood. Sand with a fine-grit sandpaper. Stain, seal, and varnish.

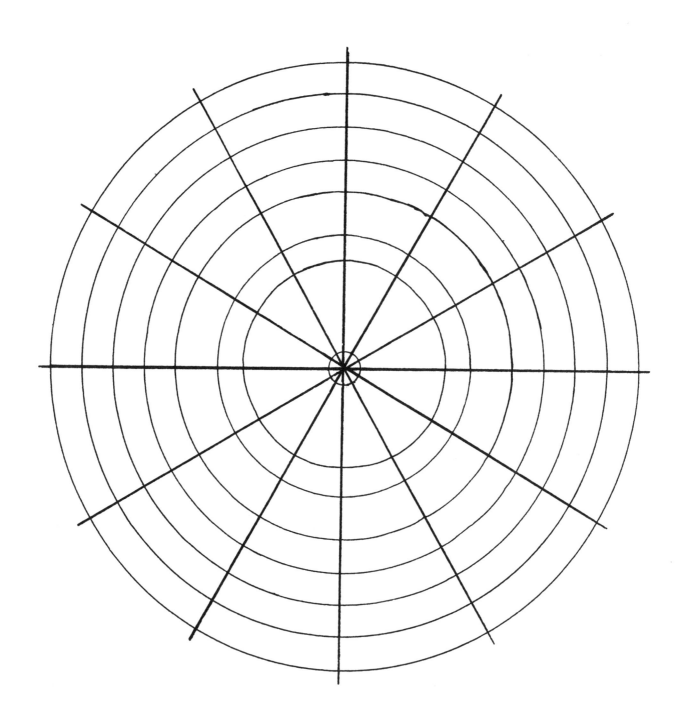

Supplies

Illus. 35. One example of a multicolor clock face.

Illus. 36. Another example of a multicolor clock face.

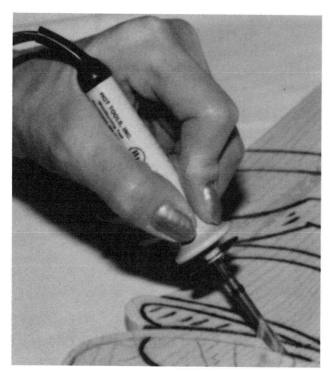

Illus. 37. Wood-burning ("hot") tool.

Illus. 40. Sawtooth hanger.

Illus. 41. Hex nut tightener.

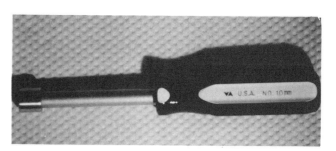

Illus. 42. Hex nut driver.

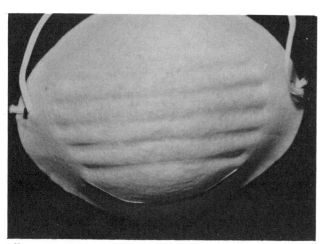

Illus. 38. Face mask/dust protector.

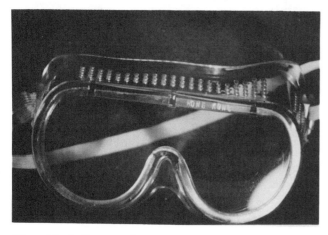

Illus. 39. Safety goggles.

Illus. 43. Ultra-thin quartz clock movement.

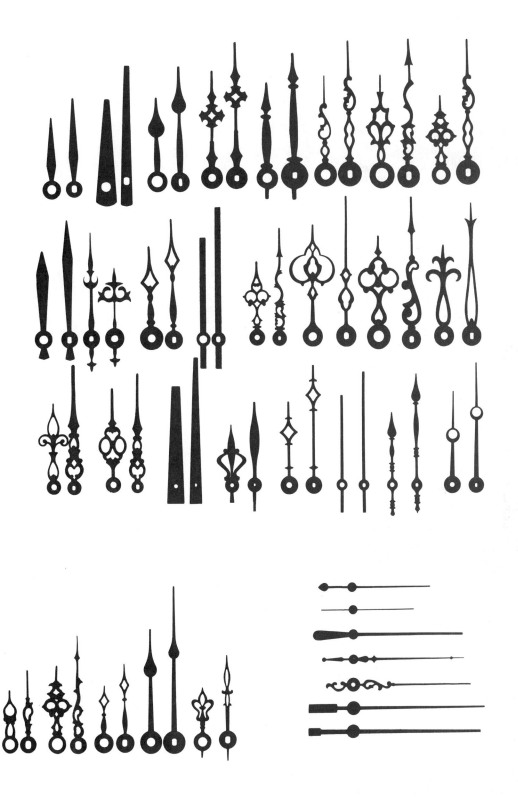

Illus. 44. Clock hands. Sweep hands (lower right).

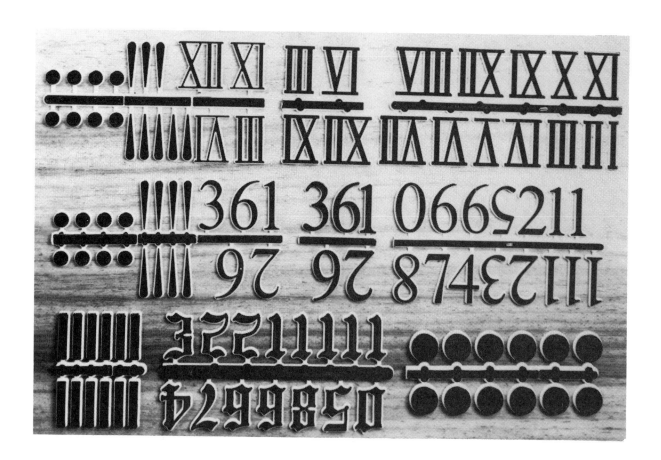

Illus. 45. Clock numerals.

101 WOODEN CLOCK PATTERNS

About the Author

Joyce Novak grew up on a farm in central Nebraska. As a child, she was fascinated by her father's workshop, and she began to use many of the woodworking tools she uses today. Later in life, her love of woodworking led her to put aside her other hobbies, and to begin to design and build wooden clocks.

Her first commission, the "tooth" clock, led to many other orders. Her clocks now hang in homes from California to New York—one even found its way to Australia. She exhibits and sells her clocks at local and regional crafts shows and county fairs. One specialty shop in California now sells her clocks, as well.

For many years a cost accounting clerk and a computer operator, she now works for a state agency. She lives in Twin Falls, Idaho.

Index